Numerical Secrets of the Bible

Numerical Secrets of the Bible
Introduction to Biblical Arithmology

by
Casper J. Labuschagne

WIPF & STOCK · Eugene, Oregon

Wipf and Stock Publishers
199 W 8th Ave, Suite 3
Eugene, OR 97401

Numerical Secrets of the Bible
Introduction to Biblical Arithmology
By Labuschagne, Casper J.
Copyright©2000 by Labuschagne, Casper J.
ISBN 13: 978-1-49892-8426-4
Publication date 7/20/2016
Previously published by Bibal Press, 2000

This was originally published with the subtitle
Rediscovering the Bible Codes.

Contents

Preface	ix
A Personal Note	xiii

1 Counting Hebrew Letters, Words, and Verses in Jewish Tradition — 1
- Introduction — 1
- The Function of Numbers in Antiquity — 5
- The Counting of Letters, Words, and Verses in the Masoretic Tradition — 7
- Seeking and Locating of the Center of the Text — 9
- The Significance of Such Counting Activities — 10
- Well-Known Numerical Compositions: the Alphabetic Poems — 12
- The Book of Lamentations as a Numerical Composition — 14
- Conclusions That Could Have Been Drawn Long Ago — 18

2 Some Significant Numbers in the Bible — 21
- A New Awareness of the Significance of Numbers in the Bible — 21
- Explicitly Mentioned Symbolic Numbers in the Bible: 40, 12, and 7 — 22
- Explicit References to the Number Seven in the Bible — 26
- The Hidden Presence of the Number Seven in the Old Testament — 31
- Examples from the Four Gospels — 33
- More Examples from Other Books of the New Testament — 33

Contents

3 Clusters and Series of Seven Divine Speeches — 41
- The Divine Speech Formulas as an Incentive to Counting — 41
- Series of Seven in the Tabernacle Laws — 42
- The Significance of the Menorah in Center Position — 48
- Series of Seven in the Book of Leviticus and the Sabbath — 49
- More Examples of Manifestly Designed Series of Seven Items — 53

4 The 7+4=11 Pattern in the Pentateuch — 57
- The Primeval History in Genesis 1–11 — 57
- The Eleven Divine Monologues in the Pentateuch — 62
- Three Genealogies in Genesis 1–11 — 64
- The Eleven *Toledoth*-Formulas in Genesis — 66
- The Role of 7 in the Life Spans of the Patriarchs — 67
- How Did 7 Acquire its Symbolic Meaning? — 69
- The Number of Fulfillment, 11 — 70

5 The Secret of the Hidden Sacred Numbers 17 and 26 — 75
- Significant Numbers in the Divine Speeches in Genesis — 75
- Examples from the Book of Exodus — 79
- Conspicuous Numbers in the Divine Speeches in Deuteronomy — 82
- Counting Verses in Deuteronomy — 85
- The Symbolic Meaning of 17 and 26 — 88
- The Divine Name Interwoven in the Fabric of the Text — 92
- The Purpose of the Hidden Numerical Structures — 93
- The Divine Name Numbers Signifying God's Presence — 96
- 17 and 26 in the Life Spans of the Patriarchs and in the Genealogies — 98
- The Watermark of the Name of God as the Hallmark of Holy Scripture — 103

Contents

6 The Bible as a High-Grade Literary Work of Art   105
   Investigating the Numerical Structure of the
      Biblical Text   105
   The Layout Markers in the Hebrew Text of Genesis   107
   The Numerical Architecture of the Hebrew Bible
      Rediscovered   111
   The Pioneering Work of Claus Schedl   114
   The Theoretical Foundations of Schedl's Thesis   117
   Schedl's Numerical Analysis of New Testament Texts   120
   Significant Compositional Models Discovered
      by Schedl   121
      a) The "Minor Tetraktys"   121
      b) The "Major Tetraktys"   127
      c) The Pentateuch- and Decalogue-Model   127
      d) The YHWH-ʾ*echad* Model   128
      e) The Numerical Menorah-Structure and the
         Balance-Model   130
   Keywords Determining the Number of Words
      in a Text   135

7 Proper Use and Misuse of Numbers   141
   The Significance of the Numerical Aspects
      of the Bible   141
   How Numerical Structures Support the
      Message of a Text   143
      a) Psalm 82   143
      b) Psalm 8   145
      c) Psalm 19   147
      d) Isa 8:19 – 9:6   149
   The Misuse of Numbers by Numerologists   153
   A Theological Assessment of the Numerical
      Aspects of the Bible   157
Notes   163
About the Author   183
Index of Scripture Citations   185

Preface

Through the ages no literary work has received so much attention as the Bible, which has been handed down from generation to generation so carefully, studied so diligently and commented upon so thoroughly. Many avenues of its writings have been explored and numerous aspects investigated in detail. Especially during the past century biblical scholars have devoted much time and energy in addressing the many questions, both literary and historical, raised by this complicated body of literature. One would think that by now the Bible must have yielded all its secrets. Yet nothing is less true, judged by the discovery in recent times of a virtually undetected and practically unknown facet of the biblical writings.

This discovery concerns a hitherto unrecognized principle of composition: the use of specific numbers in the organization and formation of the text of the canonical books of the Bible. Scholarly research the last couple of decades led to the conclusion that the biblical writings are numerical compositions. This means that they were not written off the cuff, but carefully devised and meticulously composed and structured with the help of certain numbers. These numbers have a specific symbolic meaning, on the basis of which they seem to have been used to deepen and enhance the meaning of the text. Since I have been deeply involved personally in the discovery of the numerical aspects of the Bible, I intend to take the readers on an exploratory expedition in order to let them discover for themselves what has been uncovered in this respect.

Preface

The people responsible for handing down the canonical books of the Old Testament confront us with the fascinating phenomenon of counting verses, words, and letters. We shall survey the striking occurrence of certain explicitly mentioned numbers in both the Old Testament and the New Testament. Moreover, exploring the structure of the text more deeply, we shall become aware of the exceptionally high frequency of a limited number of extremely holy numerical symbols, representing God's name and presence, woven into the very fabric of the text of Scripture. We shall become acquainted with the fascinating world of the biblical writers and with the way in which they constructed their literary compositions with great professional skill and craftsmanship.

The present book was not written for specialists. As a matter of fact, apart from a few tyros, including myself, there are no scholars with any specialized knowledge of these matters; for this is a completely new field of study. The book is intended for everyone who is interested in the Bible as literature, regardless whether the reader is a professional scholar or a lay reader, Jew or Christian, churchgoer or not. The reader might find some pages a bit technical—which was unavoidable—but I have tried to use clear and comprehensible language.

A previous version of the book was published in Dutch under the title *Vertellen met Getallen: Functie en symboliek van getallen in de bijbelse oudheid* in 1992 and has since then been reprinted. The publisher, Uitgeverij Boekencentrum, has kindly given me permission to publish it in English. Since I was free to bring about whatever changes I deemed necessary or desirable, and to add more detail, the present version is a total rewrite.

I am indebted to Professor Duane L. Christensen and Dr. William R. Scott, who showed interest in the book and willingness to include it in the publications of BIBAL Press. Duane Christensen, one of those Old Testament scholars who have come to realize that biblical study can benefit from taking the numerical aspects of the Bible seriously, has worked through

Preface

my translation and offered several valuable suggestions. Moreover, he brought my English to a higher level. For all this I wish to thank him most sincerely.

The present edition is a reprint of the 2008 version, in which I have corrected a few mistakes.

I owe thanks to Crispin Fletcher Louis and Tato Sumantri for having persued the reprinting of my book.

Haren, The Netherlands.
Winter 2015/2016.

A Personal Note

When I began to carry out my scholarly investigations into the numerical aspects of the Bible from approximately 1981 onwards, I was not sufficiently aware of the recent upsurge in kabbalistic mathematical exercises, number speculations, and other types of numerological practices and number juggling. Neither did I realize how deeply sceptical the biblical scholarly world was about numerical matters in general. What I could not sense either, was the danger of being associated with such unscholarly practices and having my work rejected out of hand. With hindsight, one of the mistakes I made in the beginning was that I failed to demarcate my numerical research at the outset clearly from these dubious numerological activities. It was only ten years later, in the Dutch version of the present book, that I dissociated myself explicitly from such practices. It is hard to say whether that would have changed the course of events.

What I did not realize and could not possibly foresee, was that the plain fact of my embarking on numerical research would put my scholarly reputation at risk and that I would be sidetracked from the inner circle of serious biblical scholarship. Knowing what happened to the Austrian orientalist and biblical scholar Claus Schedl during the sixties and seventies, whose numerical investigations were greeted with ridicule on the part of colleagues and summarily rejected, I was naively confident that the evidence I presented would enjoy favorable acceptance. However, I was faced with a very different reality from the outset by the totally unexpected negative reaction by two British scholars, P. R. Davies and D. M. Gunn, to my

A Personal Note

presentation of the numerical patterns of the Divine Speech Formulas in the Pentateuch in 1982.[1]

I was sobered up particularly by the adverse response on the part of the majority of my colleagues to the two papers I read in the summer of 1983, the first at an international Deuteronomy Conference in Louvain (Belgium), and the second at the Eleventh Congress of the International Organization for the Study of the Old Testament in Salamanca (Spain).[2]

In Louvain I was rather rudely reproached by the chairman of the session: "Do you want to lead us back to the Kabbalah?" After the lecture, only one Deuteronomy scholar, Duane Christensen, approached me to discuss my paper. Another colleague shook my hand saying: "Thanks for the lesson in mathematics, but I don't believe you!"

During my lecture in Salamanca, my wife and son, who were in the audience, counted no less than eleven attendants at the session who left the hall rather demonstratively. Some of them crumpled up my handouts and threw them on the floor. The tone of the discussion following the presentation of the paper was set by a colleague who expressed his disappointment that a reputed scholar could get himself involved in such futile activities. My work was greeted with such disbelief and contempt that I began to realize that it was destined to be ridiculed and dismissed.

After the session, I found myself completely alone, standing there on the square, out of earshot surrounded by groups of gesticulating colleagues obviously discussing the problem of Labuschagne. Nobody wanted to talk to me or to be seen in my company. There was one exception: the next day, during an excursion to Avila, a Jewish scholar laid his hand gently upon my arm and whispered the following words, which I would cherish during the years to come: "The ways of the Almighty are wonderful. To think that, after goys like Wellhausen and his followers had dissected the Torah, He once again uses a goy to open our eyes to its unity."

A Personal Note

It was in Salamanca that I fathomed the significance of the word outcast, and during the years that followed, I would also perceive what it means to be held up as an object of ridicule behind one's back. However, there was no doubt in my mind that if this was the price I had to pay for a scholarly discovery I believed in and considered significant, I was fully prepared to pay dearly. Any alternative would mean sacrificing my scholarly conscience. Therefore, despite the expectation among some of my colleagues that I would come to my senses and stop such activities, I confidently persisted in pursuing my numerical research, encouraged by what I discovered all along.

What I am presenting in this book is only a fraction of my discoveries, and merely the tip of the iceberg of undetected secrets of the biblical text. I have no illusions about any immediate effect my pleas may have on biblical scholars, but I do have confidence in the convincing power of truth on the basis of the massive amount of evidence I hereby lay on their desks.

Counting Hebrew Letters, Words, and Verses in Jewish Tradition

Introduction

The purpose of this book is to give an account of the discovery I regard as one of the most important findings of our time in the field of biblical studies: the insight that the biblical writings are numerical compositions. The numerical aspects of the text of the Bible have remained almost completely unobserved until recently, when investigations into the design of the texts shed unexpected new light upon the way they were constructed. It appears that the biblical text was *composed* according to preconceived models and patterns shaped by certain numbers that regulate the amount of words, sentences, and verses.

Specific numbers were used to forge the structure of the text in its different component parts. Like musical compositions, which are artistically constructed and arranged with the help of rhythm and melody, so literary texts in biblical antiquity were composed and structurally organized with the help of certain numbers. In short, the art of writing practiced by the biblical writers seems to have involved compositional techniques inextricably bound up with counting.

By studying the numerical aspects of the texts, we can uncover and bring to light important facets of their structure that have been forgotten or have remained hidden. Using this as a key to unlock the secrets of the formation of the texts, we are able to "decompose" them and to discover their precise organization. In biblical study, such an operation, is called *numerical structural analysis,* or *logotechnical analysis,* or *quantative structural analysis.*[1]

It stands to reason that the results of such an analysis have far-reaching consequences, not only for our view of the form and the history of the biblical texts, but also for their interpretation. As a matter of fact, form and content are closely interrelated, as we shall demonstrate in due course.

At this point in time (July 2016) the entire Hebrew Bible (Genesis-Chronicles) has been analyzed, showing that the biblical writings are meticulously designed numerical compositions. This means that the numerical features of these texts simply cannot be ignored any longer. See www.labuschagne.nl.

Discoveries in this respect have opened up new avenues for scholarly research particularly in the books of the Bible. However, other writings should be included in the investigations and studied with regard to eventual numerical aspects, such as the Samaritan Pentateuch and other ancient manuscripts witnessing to the text of the Bible as well as the ancient translations. Also still to be addressed are the many historical problems regarding the use of numbers as a compositional device in biblical antiquity. At what time did such compositional techniques arise? To what extent were they employed and for what purpose? Are they limited to and specific for the canonical books of the Bible, or were they also used for the composition of other literature, such as the deutero-canonical and pseudepigraphical books and other contemporary and early post-biblical Jewish literature? Do numerical compositional devices occur in non-Jewish literature? If so, what is specific about the books of the Bible and what are their characteristic numerical features?

Another question is how did it happen that the precise knowledge of the recently discovered numerical compositional techniques fell into oblivion, and how could the numerical aspects of the biblical books have remained hidden until their discovery in our time? The most plausible answer to this question is, in my opinion, that we are confronted with a rather esoteric compositional technique, a skill known only to insiders, the scribes. As a result of the continuous series of catastrophes suffered by the Jewish people, culminating in the annihilation of Jewish life in Palestine and resulting in the dispersion of the Jews and their persecution through the ages, the precise knowledge of this scribal secret fell into oblivion. What was handed down in Jewish tradition were vague reminiscences still reflected in the Kabbalah, more particularly in the gematria based on the principle that each letter of the Hebrew alphabet has a numerical value. This esoteric Jewish tradition did not originate as late as the Middle Ages but goes back to early Judaism, as Gershom Scholem has argued, and has its roots squarely in the biblical texts, as Claus Schedl has shown.[3]

The main reason for writing this book at a stage in which scholarly numerical research is still in an initial phase, is that I want to make it clear from the outset that the study of the numerical aspects of the Bible is a serious scientific discipline. It has nothing to do with number mysticism, numerology or juggling with numbers. Neither does it aim at leading us back to kabbalistic speculations. Its only objective is to recover the literary structure of the biblical texts and to shed new light on the compositional techniques used by the writers.

The reactions elicited by the publication of my first discoveries and preliminary findings in this respect showed that readers are apt to associate the study of the numerical aspects of the Bible with the hazy world of mysticism and magic, suggesting that such research should not be taken seriously. I realized that the pursuit of numerical studies ran the risk of being condemned beforehand as pseudo-science. On the one hand, biblical scholars, who were not interested in logotechnical research, used this as a pretext to shut their eyes to the findings and to subject such research to general ridicule. On the other hand, numerologists and number-jugglers tried to grab the results of serious numerical research and to use them for their own purposes to legitimize their pseudo-scientific practices. Moreover, fundamentalists, who believe in the mechanical divine inspiration of Scripture, claimed the discovery of the complicated numerical structures of the biblical writings as proof of the divine origin of the Bible, arguing that human beings are unable to produce such high-grade compositions.[4]

Therefore, what I envisage is to safeguard scholarly investigations into the numerical aspects of the Bible against unfounded imputations and to protect it from abuse. I intend to do so by making clear what numerical research is all about and to let the facts regarding the structural use of numbers in biblical times speak for themselves. The numerous examples I present as evidence to illustrate the extent of the use of numbers as a structuring device by the biblical writers can be checked and verified by any reader with a basic knowledge of Hebrew and Greek. It will become clear that numbers are basically pure, exact, and free of any inherent mysticism or magic. This does not rule out the fact that symbolic value could have been attached to numbers in biblical times, which unfortunately led to their use in early post-biblical mysticism and in medieval magical practices, as witnessed especially by the Kabbalah. However, such uses of numbers are definitely later phenomena, which must be regarded as secondary developments, aberrations clearly deviating from the use made of them in biblical antiquity.

The Function of Numbers in Antiquity

An examination of studies on the use of numbers in biblical times from the first half of the twentieth century, shows that these studies have themselves contributed much to the linking of numbers with mysticism and magic. A typical example is the frequently cited book by F. Dornseiff, *Das Alphabet in Mystik und Magie* (Berlin, 1925).[5] The result was that the function of numbers in biblical times came to be associated primarily with number-symbolism, number-mysticism and magic—a most unfortunate and lamentable development. Countering this deplorable situation, the primary concern of the logotechnical analysis of the biblical writings is to study the use of numbers as a *purely technical device* in the art of writing to give structure to the text. It is an exact and rational approach to the text. Nonetheless, since numbers did have a symbolic value in antiquity, the investigation into the numerical aspects of the text inevitably involves the study of the symbolism of the numbers in question as well. Study of the pure technical function of numbers in the Bible has until now been grossly neglected; for scholars seem to have been interested in their symbolic function only and in their use in mysticism and magic.[6]

In order to study the pure technical function of numbers in biblical times, scholarly research requires us to distance ourselves from the traditional association of numbers with the hazy world of mysticism, magic and pseudo-science. This means that we have to concentrate on their two main functions: first, as a technique to count, calculate and structure—also with regard to the composition of texts—and second, as a means of adding depth to a text and to imbue it with symbolic significance. As everyone knows, numbers had a symbolic value in antiquity. Therefore they had a metaphorical and allegorical capacity to refer to something beyond the surface meaning.

In our modern, rationalistic First World culture, we seem to know numbers only in their arithmetical and mathematical functions, as a means to count, reckon and measure. Though we are aware of the fact that numbers play an important role in composing music, the function of numbers in composing texts has fallen into oblivion. In addition to this, biblical scholars, being primarily schooled in arts and humanities, seem to feel ill at ease and out of their depth when it comes to numbers. This shows that though illiteracy has generally been conquered in our culture, mathematical illiteracy is still rife—even among academic scholars.[7]

Classical scholars and medieval specialists have long been acquainted with the use of numbers as a device to give structure to literary compositions. Substantial research has been carried out already regarding the structural function of symbolic numbers in classical and medieval texts, showing that numerical techniques were generally employed to organize literary compositions from antiquity until at least the eighteenth century. Numerical criticism is an accepted scholarly approach in text analysis.

> Numerological criticism analyses literary structures of various kinds, ordered by numerical symmetries or expressing number symbolism. In poetry, numerological structure often forms a level of organization intermediate in scale and externality between metrical patterns, on the one hand, and structure as ordinarily understood, on the other. As such, it constitutes a huge subject—perhaps even larger than most medieval and Renaissance scholars have begun to realize. It is probably no exaggeration to say that most good literary works—indeed, most craftsmanlike works—were organized at this stratum from antiquity until at least the eighteenth century. Moreover, numerological criticism is potentially a more fruitful subject than large-scale prosody, since it has more bearing on meaning, thematic content, structure and other adjacent strata.[8]

To what extent the biblical writers employed numerical techniques to give structure to their texts has not yet been studied systematically. In this respect, biblical scholars are lagging far behind their colleagues in classical and medieval study. This is rather surprising, if not astounding, since there have always been clear indications that biblical writers did not write their literary productions off the cuff, but composed them with care, using a variety of compositional principles.

The Counting of Letters, Words, and Verses In the Masoretic Tradition

As every student familiar with the text of the Hebrew Bible knows, the Masoretes and other copiers who were responsible for the handing down of the text of the Old Testament carefully *counted verses, words, and even letters* of the biblical books. Moreover, they painstakingly *sought, located, and marked the mathematical center* of the books, or groups of books. And, apart from their introduction of vowel signs to secure the correct pronunciation of the words that were originally written with consonants only, they brought about different kinds of spaces in the text to indicate how the text was organized in larger and smaller literary units. Finally they divided the text into reading units, *sederim* and *parashoth*, according to two systems, the Palestinian and the Babylonian, in view of the Scripture reading in the synagogue.

Below the text and in the margin they recorded "statistical" information regarding the occurrence of important or difficult words and phrases. Though deficient and incomplete, this information is nevertheless interesting because it attests to the importance attached by the Masoretes to the frequency in which words or phrases occur in a particular book. This and other information is found in scholarly printed editions of the text of the Hebrew Bible, such as the standard critical edition, *Biblia Hebraica Stuttgartensia*. The precise way in which these notes were written in the manuscript on which the printed editions are based, can be observed by anyone who examines Codex B 19^A, generally known as the *Leningrad Codex*. This manuscript, the oldest complete hand-written manuscript of the text of the Hebrew Bible (dating from 1008 or 1009 CE), which is housed in the Russian National Library in St. Petersburg (formerly Leningrad), is now available in a superb facsimile edition for any student of the Bible to examine.⁹

To give an example of the statistical information: at the end of the book of Genesis there is a note saying:

> The sum of the verses of the book:
> one-thousand-five-hundred-thirty-four
> 1534

And in Gen 27:40, the center of the book of Genesis is marked with a marginal note calling attention to the words that Isaac says to Jacob: ועל־חרבך תחיה "By your sword you will live." On the level of verses this verse forms the mathematical center of the book, which has been marked at the appropriate place in the text.

The total number of verses, 1534, happens to be a multiple of the extremely important and particularly holy number 26 (59×26), representing the numerical value of the Tetragrammaton, the four letters of the divine name יהוה *YHWH*, which signifies his presence. The numerical value is based upon the position of the four letters in the Hebrew alphabet: (י=10) + (ה=5) + (ו=6) + (ה=5) = 26. We shall examine the significance and function of this number in detail below.

Contrary to what we would have expected, there is no statement of the number of words and letters in Genesis—neither is there such a statement in the books of Exodus, Leviticus, Numbers or Deuteronomy. However, a note to this effect appears at the end of Deuteronomy, i.e., at the end of the five books of the Torah:

> Sum of the verses of the Torah: 5845
> Sum of the words of the Torah: 79,856
> Sum of the letters of the Torah: 400,945

What is significant about these numbers is that the first two are a multiple of 7 (5845 = 7×835; 79,856 = 7×11,408) and the last one a multiple of 17 (400,945 = 17×23,585). Next to 26, the number 17 is the other particularly important and holy number, which is also associated with the name YHWH (see chapter 5, under the heading "The Symbolic Meaning of 17 and 26").

Seeking and Locating the Center of the Text

As in the case of the book of Genesis and the masoretic note about the central verse of that book, such centers have been located in the other books of the Pentateuch as well. Thus the verse in the absolute middle of the book of Exodus is 22:27, in Leviticus it is 15:7, in Numbers 17:20 (in some translations 17:5) and in Deuteronomy 17:10. The statements concerning the mathematical center of the Torah on the level of verses, words and letters do not occur at the end of the Pentateuch but can be found at the relevant places in the margin.

- The center of the Torah on verse level is Lev 8:8, where it is said: "He (Moses) put the breastpiece on him (Aaron) and set the Urim and Thummim in it."
- The center of the Torah on word level is in Lev 10:16, *darosh darash,* "He (Moses) made searching inquiry."
- The center of the Torah on letter level is the *w* (= *o*) of the word גחון (*gachon*), "belly," in Lev 11:42, indicated by a dot above the *w* (*waw*) and by the fact that the *w* is written somewhat larger than the other letters.

Statements of the number of verses in a particular book and a note indicating its center can be found with regard to the other books of the Old Testament as well. Without going into any further details, we may draw the following conclusions on the basis of the fact that the people responsible for the transmission of the text of the Hebrew Bible meticulously counted and registered the verses, words, and letters of the texts and located their mathematical center. First, they committed themselves to counting, because they knew that counting had something to do with the biblical text. Second, the fact that they looked for and located the mathematical center of a book or a group of books shows that for some reason they attached importance to knowing the location of the center of a text.

The Significance of Such Counting Activities

Scholars have always been aware of the fact that verses, words, and letters were counted and some results registered in the transmission process of the text of the Hebrew Bible. The traditional explanation biblical scholars have always given for this remarkable phenomenon was that counting was used as an instrument to control whether the text was copied correctly when new copies were made. However, when we weigh this answer critically, we have to admit that it does not offer a satisfactory explanation. By counting, only one thing can be checked, and that is the correctness of the total number of words in the text, no more than that. It simply cannot guarantee that the text was copied faultlessly. Even if the total number of words are correct, words could have been spelled incorrectly or transposed; a word could have been left out in one place, and at another point in the text a word could have been written double. The correctness of a new copy can only be controlled by a word-for-word check.

There must be a better and more satisfactory answer. Moreover, we have to look for an answer that can explain other phenomena as well, namely the painstaking locating and registering of the center of the text. As far as I am aware, scholars have always disregarded this curious phenomenon. They seem to have been at a loss to explain this aspect of the transmission process of the text. In any case, the two phenomena were never viewed together and explained in conjunction with each other.

What I propose is to explain both phenomena in light of the discovery that the biblical writings are numerical compositions and that the people responsible for the transmission of the text were, in some way or other, aware of this. As I shall demonstrate and substantiate with examples below, counting was part and parcel of the art of writing in biblical antiquity as a device to give structure to the text.

One of the techniques commonly used was to organize the contents of a text in such a way that the most important element was situated in the mathematical center position. A good example is Psalm 23, which we shall study more closely later. There the three words in the phrase *ki ʾatta ʿimmadi*, "for you are with me" (23:4), are situated in the mathematical center of the text, with 26 words preceding them and 26 after them. The structure of the text, formed according to an often used model, the balance-model: 26 + 3 + 26, signifies that the statement about the *presence* of God is a central and crucial element in the psalm. Seeing that 26 represents the divine name YHWH, and therefore his presence, I interpret the message encoded in the structure of the Psalm as an affirmation of the poet's conviction that God is all around him. This is perfectly in line with what is said of God in Ps 139:5, "You keep close guard behind me and before me."

In light of this, we can imagine that the disturbance of the numerical organization of a text would mean the changing of its structure as a means of underscoring and enhancing its message. Therefore, in order to keep such purposeful and meaningful structures of the text intact, it was of paramount importance in the transmission process to preserve its numerical aspects. This was, in my opinion, the real reason behind the counting of the verses, words, and letters of the biblical texts and the seeking and locating of their mathematical center.

During the transmission of the text of the Hebrew Bible through the centuries, the precise knowledge of the numerical compositional techniques employed in the biblical writings fell into oblivion. Nevertheless the counting of verses, words, and letters and the locating of the center of texts continued. This happened no longer on the basis of intimate knowledge of their precise structure, but on the basis of vague reminiscence of the importance of its numerical aspects. It should be kept in mind that it concerns a specialized craftsmanship. In the course of time, such expertise, known only to a limited number of people, could easily be lost sight of and forgotten, until its rediscovery in recent times.

Well-Known Numerical Compositions
The Alphabetic Poems

Certain texts in the Old Testament that are unmistakable numerical compositions, the so-called alphabetic poems, have been a constant reminder that biblical texts were not written off the cuff, but were artistically composed according to premeditated patterns and models. In its most simple form, the alphabetic poem is structured on the basis of the twenty-two letters of the Hebrew alphabet, consisting of 22 lines, verses, or groups of verses. The first letter of the first word of each line represents a letter of the alphabet in succession in the traditional order, from the ʾaleph to the taw. Unfortunately in most modern translations this typical structure of the alphabetic acrostics is not shown. In the *King James Version*, however, the text of Psalm 119 is divided into groups of verses following the letters of the alphabet.

A good example of this type of poem is found in the twin psalms 111 and 112, which are closely connected in terms of form and content. Both have the heading *Hallelu-Yah*; both consist of 22 lines divided over 10 verses, in such a way that the first eight verses have two lines each while verses 9 and 10 have three lines each. Psalm 111 with its 72 words and Psalm 112 with its 77 words comprise together 149 words, but including the 4 words of their headings the total number of words comes to 153 (9×17). This is a very significant number, being the sum of the numbers 1–17, well-known from the 153 fish referred to in John 21:11, symbolically signifying all the nations gathered into the kingdom of God. Moreover, in accordance with the principle that the 22 letters of the Hebrew alphabet have numerical value, 153 is the numerical value of the Hebrew words בני האלהים "the children of God" (ב =2)

Counting Hebrew Letters, Words, and Verses

+ (נ=50) + (י=10) + (ה=5) + (א=1) + (ל=30) + (ה=5) + (י=10) + (מ=40) = 153.[10]

What is significant about Psalm 112 is that the total number of words (77) is a multiple of two structuring numbers, 11 and 7. Moreover, since verses in the Bible are divided into two halves by the verse-divider *'atnach*, the verses in this psalm are so divided that there are 44 (4×11) words before and 33 (3×11) after the divider, showing that 11 was intentionally used as a structuring number. In Psalm 111, there are *41* words before and *31* after the divider, bringing the total in the two poems to 85 (5 ×17) words before and *64* after the divider. Reading the two psalms in translation, one would never notice the strict alphabetic and numerical form of the text behind the natural flow of words. It is only when one consults the original Hebrew text that one can detect the alphabetic structure, and only when one counts and assesses the number of their words can one uncover their numerical structure.

The compositional technique employed in the alphabetic poem not only gives structure to the text, but also serves as a mnemonic device to facilitate the learning and recitation of the poem. The alphabetical structure was intended to have a symbolic function: to connote the totality of expressiveness by using all the letters of the alphabet to express what is said in the text. In terms of music, for instance: opening all the registers of the organ.

Other examples of the alphabetic poem are found in Psalm 37 and Prov 31:10–31. It appears in its most extensive form in Psalm 119, consisting of 176 one-line verses divided into 22 blocks of *eight* verses, each beginning with the same letter of the alphabet. This means that in addition to the normal 22 alphabetic verses the poet produced 22 times *seven* extra verses beginning with the same letter: 22×7 = 154. Since 7 is the number expressing fullness and abundance, as will be illustrated in the next two chapters, the purpose of using this number was obviously to enhance the already exuberant praise of the Torah in the psalm symbolically, amplifying them to extreme fullness. So to speak, here all the registers of praise were opened *sevenfold*.

On the level of *verses*, the mathematical center of Psalm 119 with its 176 verses is between verse 88 and 89, dividing the psalm into 88 verses before and 88 verses after this center. Most significantly, a count of the *words* of the psalm (a total of 1063) brings to light that the mathematical center on word level is situated at the very same place. It is constituted by the three words at the end of verse 88, *we'eshmera 'edut pika*, "that I may follow the instruction of your mouth," showing a balance-model (which we have already encountered in Psalm 23): 530 + 3 + 530. This means that the mathematical center on *word* level corresponds with the mathematical center on *verse* level. That the two coincide bears witness to the compositional craftsmanship of the author of this psalm.

The Book of Lamentations as a Numerical Composition

Please visit my website for a more in-depth numerical structural analysis of Lamentations.

The number **154** (7×22), which we encountered above, the product of the number of fullness **7** and **22**, the number of letters in the alphabet (and incidentally 14×11, the number of fulfillment), also occurs in the book of Lamentations, another example of a conspicuous numerical composition in the Old Testament. This fascinating booklet with its **154** Masoretic verses is structured consistently by the idea of the **22** letters of the alphabet. It comprises five chapters, with chapter 3 in the mathematical center—which, with its 66 verses, has strikingly three times the 22 verses of the surrounding four chapters.

In terms of poetic verselines, we get a different picture: chapter 1 and 2 have 67 verselines each, [11] while chapter 4 has 44 and chapter 5 has 22. Moreover, chapters 1 and 2 stand out as having only 22 (initial) alphabetic verselines each (with 45 non-alphabetic verselines). Chapter 3 on the other

Counting Hebrew Letters, Words, and Verses

hand, is made up of 3×22 = 66 *one*-line alphabetic verselines, in which every letter of the alphabet occurs three times as initial letter in each verse.

Chapters	Verses	Verselines	Words
1	22	67 (22 alphabetic, 45 not)	374 (17×22) [see note 11]
2	22	67 (idem)	381 [see note 11]
3	66	66 (22 sets of 3 alphabetic)	381
4	22	44 (22 alphabetic, 22 not)	259
5	22	22 (22 sets of 1 alphabetic)	145
Totals:	154 (7×22)	264 (12×22)	1540 (70×22)

What has been said above about the symbolic function of the structural numbers 7 and 22, applies here as well, but now with regard to the affliction of the people and the passionate expression of grief for them: the number **22** and its multiples signify that the registers of lament are opened *sevenfold*, on Masoretic verse level, *twelvefold* on verseline level, and *seventyfold* on word level.

Chapter 3 not only forms the mathematical center of the book on the level of chapters: 1–2 + **3** + 4–5, but also on the level of Masoretic verses: 44 + **66** + 44. Moreover, from the perspective of content, chapter 3 constitutes the turning point in the book. The *mathematical center* of this central chapter is to be found in 3:25–42, comprising *six* sets of three-line verses. Here the leading theme, already intimated in verses 19–24, is no longer lament, but hope, self-examination, and conversion based upon Yahweh's mercy. This center can be delimited precisely. It starts most significantly with a threefold use of the key word *tob*, "good," in verses 25, 26, and 27, and ends with a striking shift from third to second person, addressing Yahweh directly, in verse 42, as is also the case in the next section 3:43–45.

The Masoretes located the *mathematical center of the book* on the level of *verses* between verses 33 and 34—in the Leningrad Codex at the indentation at the beginning of verse 34. At this point, not only the 18 verses of *3:25–42* but also *chapter 3*, with its 66 verses, and the *whole book*, with its **154** verses, are all divided into two equal halves:

18 = 9+9 verses, and **66** = 33+33 verses in the center, and **154** = 77+77 in the book.

With the 18 Masoretic verses of 3:25–42 at the *center* of both chapter 3 and the book as a whole, the entire text appears to have a typical *sevenfold* structure in a *menorah* pattern, of which I shall give many examples later:

1.	1:1–22	22 verses		
2.	2:1–22	22 verses	}	**68** (4x17) Masoretic verses
3.	3:1–24	24 verses		
4.	3:25–42			**18 verses — mathematical center**
5.	3:43–66	24 verses		
6.	4:1–22	22 verses	}	**68** (4x17) Masoretic verses
7.	5:1–22	22 verses		

The 18-verse center is flanked by *three* branches consisting of **68** (4×**17**) verses on each side, which clearly demonstrates once again the use of the holy number **17**.

An examination of the center itself on the level of *words* reveals that it is likewise structured by the number **17**. The 6-word verse **34** at the mathematical center is flanked by **51** (3×**17**) words on either side, and surrounded by **17** Masoretic verses (9 + 8):

3:25–33	51 words (3×17)		9 verses	
3:34	6 words	1 verse		} 17 verses.
3:35–42	51 words (3×17)		8 verses	

This structure can hardly be a matter of chance and must be reckoned with in interpreting the book. It means, in any case, that both centers, 3:25–42, and 3:34 should receive special attention. The leading theme of the central section is not lamentation and wailing but hope, self-examination, and conversion based upon Yahweh's mercy. Note also that the "trampling underfoot of all the prisoners of the earth" (v. 34a) is the first thing Yahweh does not approve.

Like Psalm 23 and 119, the book of Lamentations is an example of the meticulously organized structure of biblical texts, of the important function of the numbers **17** and **26** as a structuring device, and of the significance of the mathematical center of a text. I will illustrate these three aspects later in more detail, but at this stage I would sound a note of warning. We should not expect that every text in the Bible has been structured with the help of the divine Name numbers, nor should we suppose to find a mathematical center in every text. A text can certainly lack such a center and need not be structured necessarily by divine Name numbers. Other numerical characteristics are possible.

Though what has been said above on the structure and content of the book of Lamentations must suffice,[12] I would call attention to another interesting feature in this book: the *acrostics* in chapter 5:1–4 and 19–22. The acrostic is a technique used to form a name, word, or phrase with the first letters of successive lines or verses of a text to "encode" a message in it. The alphabetic poems are in fact *alphabetic acrostics*.

In chapter 5, the author of Lamentations abandoned the principle of the *alphabetic* acrostic but retained the regular number of 22 verses.[13] Instead of the alphabetic acrostic, he employed another type of acrostic, using, so far as we can see, not all but only some initial letters. Such an acrostic can be detected in 5:1–4 where the initial letters of the four verses, *z n y m*, spell the word *zonim*, "adulterers." The word obviously refers to the unfaithfulness of the Israelites in their relationship with God (see also Hosea 4:15).

Significantly enough the total number of words in 5:1–4 is **26** (9 in vs. 1 and **17** in vss. 2–4). The numbers **17** and **26** appear to have been used intentionally as a device to "seal" the passage, giving it special emphasis and accentuating Yahweh's *presence*.

Another acrostic appears in 5:19–22, where the initial letters of these four verses spell the word *aeloheka*, "your God." This passage, consisting of *28* words—which does not seem to have a special symbolic significance—contains an urgent appeal to

God to mend and restore his relationship with his people. The acrostic clearly functions to stress the fact that Yahweh is still Israel's God, in spite of their apostasy. However, such acrostic devices were used on a small scale, since they have been detected in a limited number of instances only.[14]

Once again it should be stressed that such "coded messages" are very sparse in the Bible. In this respect, a stern warning against Bible freaks using the computer to detect supposed hidden predictions in the biblical text, is necessary and appropriate. See my remarks in chapter 7 under the heading "The Misuse of Numbers by Numerologists."

Conclusions That Could Have Been Drawn Long Ago

Evaluating the evidence adduced above, we may wonder why evidently numerical compositions such as the alphabetic acrostics have not been studied more carefully with regard to their numerical aspects, and why biblical scholars have turned a blind eye in general to the numerical aspects of the biblical text. Though there has always been a vague awareness among scholars that there is something significant about numbers in the Bible, the biblical writings in general have not been studied with regard to their numerical aspects.

That the Masoretes diligently *counted* verses, words, and letters—something we have known all along—should have made us appreciate such counting and should have opened our eyes to the significance of counting. The fact that the Masoretes attached great importance to seeking and locating the center of the biblical writings on the level of verses, words, and letters *by counting*, should have led us to realize that the mathematical center of texts has relevance to their structure. Moreover, in view of the fact that the biblical writers used the 22 letters of the alphabet to give structure to acrostic poems, an operation that involved *counting* we should have drawn the conclusion long ago that numbers were used in the composition of texts and that *specific* numbers imbued these texts at the same time with symbolic meaning. However, it was only in recent times that biblical scholars began to appreciate the significance of numbers as a compositional principle to give structure to a text and imbue it with a specific symbolism. How I myself came to realize that counting was part and parcel of the art of writing in biblical antiquity forms the substance of the following chapters.

Some Significant Numbers In the Bible

A New Awareness of the Significance of Numbers in the Bible

I do not intend to give a historical survey here of the emergence of what may be called a new awareness in our time of the numerical aspects of the Bible. Neither shall I try to give an answer to the question of who precisely should be credited with the honor of being the discoverer of the insight that the biblical writings are numerical compositions. In point of fact, since there has always been some awareness of the significance of numbers in the Bible, particularly in the Jewish tradition, one cannot really speak of the discovery of the numerical aspects of the Bible in our time. It is rather a matter of a rediscovery, a new and deeper awareness in recent times of the important role played by numbers as a literary structuring principle in the biblical writings. This awareness led to serious endeavors the last three decades to study the numerical aspects of the Bible on a scientific basis. This study has been done on a limited scale, since the great majority of biblical scholars still seem to be indifferent.[1]

I intend to tell how I myself became aware of the significance of numbers in biblical antiquity, and how I came to appreciate the crucial role they played in the composition of the biblical texts. In doing so, I shall describe the rise of the scholarly discipline of numerical structural analysis and refer to the work of the pioneers in this field of study.

Without claiming any break-through yet as regards the attitude of biblical scholars towards the numerical aspects of the Bible, I believe that something has changed. Since the emergence of serious scholarly research in this respect, there are signs that scholars are beginning to realize that they cannot go on ignoring these matters indefinitely. Numerical structural analysis is here to stay and the results already brought to light simply cannot be dismissed as unimportant. Up till now, scholars could shut their eyes to matters pertaining to numbers in the Bible, shrugging them off and regarding them as only relevant to mystics, numerologists, and number jugglers. However, that time has passed. Biblical scholars find themselves confronted with two options. They can continue on the old course of ignoring the facts and run the risk of being exposed ultimately as having lacked a scholarly attitude, or they can take the numerical aspects of the Bible seriously and acknowledge the facts already brought to light by the pioneers.

The latter choice entails the necessity of accepting numerical structural analysis as part and parcel of textual analysis. The reason is simple: if the biblical authors regarded counting as inextricably bound up with writing and used numbers to give structure to their literary products, we have no right to disregard the quantitative aspects of their texts. On the contrary, we must take them into account. In my experience, as I shall demonstrate, the study of the quantitative aspects of the biblical text opens up fascinating new vistas to our understanding of their structure and beauty of composition.

Explicitly Mentioned Symbolic Numbers In the Bible: 40, 12, and 7

My interest in the numerical aspects of the Bible goes back to my childhood. The daily Bible reading in our family and the Bible stories my mother told us in our private Sunday school

Some Significant Numbers in the Bible

made me familiar with the contents of Scripture. One of the things that caught my interest and fascinated me most, apart from the exceptionally high life spans of our biblical ancestors, was the high frequency in occurrence of certain numbers, particularly 40, 12 and 7.[2]

How I marveled at the fact that in the story of the Great Flood it rained for 40 days and 40 nights; that Moses is said to have spent 40 days and 40 nights on the mountain; that Elijah's journey to the mountain of Horeb took exactly 40 days and 40 nights, and that the Gospels tells us that Jesus spent 40 days and 40 nights in the desert. And is it not so that the Israelites trekked 40 years through the desert and that it took the explorers 40 days to spy out the land of Canaan?

Having heard the number 40 so frequently, I first regarded it as a matter of coincidence. But then I began to wonder as I discovered numerous other instances. The Philistine warrior Goliath challenged the Israelites for 40 days. Ezekiel is said to have lain on one side for 40 days. Jonah warned the people of Nineveh that the city would be overthrown in 40 days. The priest Eli is said to have been judge over Israel for 40 years; and David, Solomon and Joash reigned for 40 years.

As a child, I could do nothing but marvel at the frequent occurrence of the number 40, which I regarded as something belonging to the wonderful world of the Bible. It was only when I grew up and went on to study theology that I discovered that numbers can have a symbolic function. I learned that the number 40—which occurs in the Bible almost exclusively in connection with time—was used by the biblical writers to express a special, but indefinite and indeterminate span of time.[3]

Another number that struck me by its high frequency was 12, the number of the sons of Israel's ancestor Jacob. However, it is also said that Nahor, the brother of Abraham, had 12 sons; and the same goes for Ishmael, Abraham's eldest son. It did not surprise me to hear that in the wake of the twelve tribes of Israel there were 12 explorers of the land, 12 men who brought 12 stones from the Jordan to build a memorial.

Nor was I surprised to learn that the high priest wore 12 precious stones on his breast, that the Israelites found 12 springs and 70 palm trees in Elim, that there were 12 loaves of the Bread of Presence in the sanctuary, and that Moses, Joshua, and Elijah built altars of 12 stones.

It was not unexpected to learn that Jesus had 12 disciples, who would—according to Matthew 19—sit on 12 thrones to judge the 12 tribes of Israel. Rev 7:4–8 refers to the 144,000 servants of God marked with the seal: 12,000 from each of the 12 tribes. In Revelation 21, we read that the new Jerusalem will have a wall of 12 foundation-stones, with 12 gates guarded by 12 angels. It seemed only fitting to hear that, after Jesus' first wonderful feeding of the crowd, the leftovers filled 12 baskets. However, it was a bit unexpected to find out that at the second feeding the scraps filled 7 baskets, but 7 is another frequently used number that we will examine in detail below.

What is symbolically expressed by the number 12 is completeness, perfection, and totality, which was derived from the fact that 12 is the product of the factors 3 and 4, representing the vertical and the horizontal dimension of the world respectively. In the ancient Near Eastern view of the world, the cosmos consisted of 3 vertically arranged levels: the vault of the heavens, the earth, and the nether world; on the horizontal level the earth has four quarters. Thus $3 \times 4 = 12$ expresses the idea of the perfect, harmonious totality: encompassing the whole of heaven and earth. In this respect, 12 is intimately related to 7, the sum of 3 and 4, the number expressing fullness, completeness, and abundance. Moreover, it could have been known in the ancient world and in biblical antiquity that 12 is the sum of the measures of the three sides of the perfect rectangular triangle (height 3, breadth 4, and diagonal 5), and even before Pythagoras, that $(3 \times 3) + (4 \times 4) = 5 \times 5$.[4]

Since the numbers 12 and 40 do not function as text structuring numbers in the Bible, as far as I can judge at this point in time, we need not discuss their use any further. It must suffice to state that they served the purpose of demonstrating the

Some Significant Numbers in the Bible

unmistakable symbolic use of numbers in the Bible, showing clearly that we must be aware of the fact that numbers in biblical usage should not always be understood in their literal sense.

In the present context, and for my purpose to bring the structuring function of symbolic numbers in the Bible to the attention of the reader, the number 7 should be studied more closely. It was particularly this number that fascinated me most as a child when I was confronted with the contents of the Bible. What made this number special for me was not so much the fact that my parents had 7 children, but more particularly the fact that we got acquainted with this special biblical number through the daily family Bible reading. Evening after evening, we had to listen attentively to what my father read, especially because after the prayer and the singing we were called upon in turn to tell what impressed us most and to recite a striking sentence or verse. We did not realize that this was an excellent exercise in attentive listening and remembering. Our greatest concern was, as we say in Afrikaans and Dutch, not to "stand with the mouth full of teeth," unable to say a word, having forgotten what we tried to remember.

It was exciting, and sometimes even frightening, when my father read about the apocalyptic expectations in the book of Revelation. In these readings the exceptionally high frequency of the number 7 could not escape our notice. The 7 churches, the 7 stars, the scroll with its 7 seals, the lamb with 7 horns and 7 eyes, the monster with its 7 heads and 10 horns, the 7 angels, 7 trumpets, 7 plagues, 7 bowls, 7 thunderclaps . . .

Many years afterward, I learned that this particular number is explicitly mentioned no less than 56 times in the book of Revelation. Seeing its high frequency of occurrence elsewhere in the Scripture, I realized that 7 should be considered the most important symbolic number in the Bible. What I did not know at that time was that this number would be my access number to the fascinating world of the biblical numerical compositions.

Explicit References To the Number Seven in the Bible[5]

No other number has a higher score when it comes to the number of times it is mentioned explicitly in the Bible. In the great majority of instances, it does not have a literal, but clearly a symbolic meaning. Occurring no less than 390 times in the Old Testament and 88 times in the New Testament, it runs, so to speak, as a thread through many books of the Bible. This is not surprising, since it was the number *par excellence* employed to express symbolically the idea of fullness, completeness, totality, and wholeness.[6]

In ancient Israel, the number 7 is associated with the rhythm of life by giving structure to the flow of time by means of the Sabbath, the seventh day of the week. No wonder that it was also used in other ways as a structuring and organizing principle, more particularly to give structure to the content of texts and to imbue them with its symbolism, by means of series and cycles of seven, as I shall illustrate further on. It stands to reason that in such cases the number 7 is not visibly or audibly present in the text, because it is not explicitly mentioned. Its presence as a structuring device can only be detected by counting instances, items, phrases, or words: e.g., the series of seven parables in Matthew 13, the seven intentions in the prayer of Solomon in 1 Kings 8, and the seven intentions in the prayer Jesus taught his followers.

Before surveying such latent occurrences, I shall first give the reader a general impression of the many instances in which 7 is mentioned explicitly: seven and multiples of seven, sevenfold, seven times, seventy, seventy-seven, seven hundred, etc. Significantly the first explicit reference to 7 occurs in the Creation Story in the very first chapter of the Bible according to the Hebrew text, Gen 1:1 – 2:3, where it is said that on the seventh day, God, having finished all his work, blessed that day and made it holy. In Genesis 4 we read that Lamech said: "If 7-fold vengeance was to be exacted for Cain, for Lamech it would be 77-fold." In Leviticus 26, it is said no less than four times that God would punish his disobedient people "7 times over" for their sins (verses 18, 21, 24, and 28). The 7-fold vengeance reminds us not only of what is said in Ps 79:12, "Turn back 7-fold on their own heads, Lord, the contempt our neighbors pour on you," but also of Jesus' injunction: "If your brother does wrong, reprove him; and if he repents, forgive him. Even if he wrongs you 7 times in a day and comes back to you 7 times saying "I am sorry," you are to forgive him" (Luke 17:3–4). According to Matt 18:21–22, when Peter asked Jesus whether one should forgive 7 times, he said: "I do not say 7 times but 70 times 7."

In the story of the flood in Genesis 7, God commanded Noah to take with him in the ark 7 pairs "of every kind of clean animal" (7:2), and 7 pairs "of every kind of bird" (7:3). God said that in 7 days time he would send rain on the earth for 40 days and 40 nights. The ark grounded on the mountains of Ararat on the seventeenth day of the seventh month; and Noah, having sent out a dove that returned, waited 7 days more and again sent out the dove.

In the story of Jacob and Esau we are told in Genesis 33 that Jacob bowed low to the ground 7 times as he approached his brother Esau. The author of Psalm 119 declares that he praises God 7 times each day (verse 164). In Psalm 12, refined gold is called "gold purified 7 times over." In the story of Daniel, in chapter 3, it is said that King Nebuchadnezzar ordered that the furnace had to be heated to 7 times its usual heat. In Joshua 6, we are told that 7 priests carrying 7 trumpets had to go before the ark when the Israelites marched round the city of Jericho, and that they had to march round the city 7 times on the seventh day. In Prov 24:16, it is said of an upright person: "Though he may fall 7 times, he is soon up again."

There are many instances of 7 as a span of time. According to 1 Kings 6, Solomon built the temple in 7 years. In Daniel 4, we read that Nebuchadnezzar was told three times that "7 times" would pass over him. Of Ezekiel it is said that after he arrived among the exiles he stayed with them for 7 days in a state of consternation. The great famine during Elisha's life lasted 7 years (2 Kings 4). In 2 Samuel 10, it is said that after he was anointed king, Saul had to wait 7 days for further orders. Certain impurities were supposed to last for 7 days (Lev 15:19 and 28; Num 19:11, 14 and 16). A marriage feast as well as the Feast of the Unleavened Bread and the Feast of Tabernacles lasted 7 days. Passover was celebrated in the seventh month and the Feast of Weeks 7 weeks later. The Year of Jubilee, according to Leviticus 25, was celebrated after 49 (=7×7) years, in the fiftieth year.

The number 7 expressed symbolically the idea of abundance, profuseness, and completeness, especially in regard to having many children. Job had 7 sons and 3 daughters—which brings to mind Solomon's 700 wives and 300 concubines (1 Kings 11:3). Having 7 children means fecundity, as in the case of Leah (Genesis 30). In similar manner, we read in the Song of Hannah in 1 Samuel 2:5, "The barren woman bears 7 children." And Jeremiah refers to "the mother of 7 sons," i.e. a very strong woman, who sank into despair on the day of judgement. Having 7 sons was supposed to be something very special: Ruth was said to "have proved to be better than 7 sons" to her mother-in-law Naomi (4:15).

In Genesis 46 and Exodus 1, we are told that Jacob had 70 descendants in Egypt. This reminds us of the fact that in ancient Israel and in Judaism it was thought that there were 70 nations. In Numbers 11, it is said that the spirit of the Lord was conferred on 70 of Israel's elders, and in Luke 10:1 that Jesus sent 70 disciples ahead of him. And didn't God leave 7000 in Israel who have not bowed the knee to Baal (see 1 Kgs 19:18 and Rom 11:4)?

According to Deuteronomy 7, the Israelites were confronted with 7 nations, of whom it is said in Acts 13:19 that God overthrew them. In Deut 28:7, we read that it would be a blessing for the Israelites if their enemies would come by one way towards them but flee from them by 7 ways—compare verse 25, where the same image is used with regard to Israel.

The number 7, in connection with gifts and sacrifices, frequently expresses the idea of abundance. Abraham reserved 7 lambs for Abimelech as a testimony that he had dug a certain well (Gen 21:28—29). Job's three friends had to bring 7 bulls and 7 rams as a whole-offering for themselves (Job 42:8) and Balak had to build 7 altars for Balaam and prepare 7 bulls and 7 rams (Num 23:1). According to 2 Chr 29:21, 7 bulls, 7 rams, and 7 lambs were brought as a whole-offering and 7 he-goats as a purification offering. The blood of an offering and anointing oil could be sprinkled 7 times (Lev 4:6 and 8:11).

In many other instances, 7 expresses the idea of fullness and abundance. There were 7 years of bumper harvests and 7 years of famine in Egypt, symbolically represented in Pharaoh's dream by the 7 lean and 7 gaunt cows and the 7 ears of full, ripe grain and the 7 blighted, thin ears. Samson is said to have been bound with 7 fresh bowstrings and to have had 7 locks of hair (Judges 16). In Isa 4:1, the prophet refers to 7 women who would cling to one man to be enabled to bear his name. In 1 Kings 18, we read that Elijah's servant had to go and look toward the west 7 times for signs of rain and that he saw a cloud the seventh time. We are told that after Elisha revived the child of the Shunammite woman from apparent death, the boy sneezed 7 times and opened his eyes (2 Kgs 4:35). And we read that Naaman was ordered by Elisha to go and wash 7 times in the Jordan to be cured from his illness (2 Kgs 5:10)?

The house of Wisdom was supposed to have been built on 7 pillars (Prov 9:1). There are 7 steps in the approach to the new temple envisaged by Ezekiel (40:22). The golden lampstand with its six branches had 7 lamps (Exod 25:37; Num 8:1); and the lampstand the prophet saw in a vision had 7 lamps and 7 pipes (Zech 4:2). The stone set before Joshua had 7 facets (3:9) representing "the eyes of the Lord which range over the whole earth" (4:10). This brings back to memory the vision in

Rev 5:6 about the lamb with 7 horns and 7 eyes, the eyes representing "the 7 spirits of God sent to every part of the world."

We find the predilection for the number 7 in the New Testament as well as the Old Testament. In addition to the examples already cited, I would remind the reader of the following instances. In Luke 2, it is said of the old prophetess that she had been married for 7 years (i.e., a complete number of years) and lived alone as a widow to the age of 84 (7 cycles of 12 years). According to the Gospel of Mark (8:6) Jesus fed a crowd with 7 loaves of bread; this miracle was preceded, however, by a previous feeding where Jesus also used 7 items: 5 loaves and 2 fish (6:38). In both cases, 7 seems to express both the totality of what was available and the idea of sufficiency and abundance. It is no coincidence that 7 evil spirits were driven from Mary of Magdala. On another occasion, Jesus spoke about an evil spirit that comes out of a person and comes back with 7 others to settle there again (Matt 12:43–45). And in their discussion with Jesus about the resurrection, the Sadducees referred to the case involving 7 brothers who were married in succession to the same woman (Matt 22:23–28). Acts 6 tells about the appointment of 7 men of good repute to serve the church. Since I had to learn such names by heart in my childhood, I can still reproduce their names: Stephen, Philip, Prochorus, Nicanor, Timon, Parmenas and Nicolas.

The New Testament passage about these 7 men, of whom it is said that they were "full of the Spirit and of wisdom," reminds us of the messianic prophecy in Isaiah 11, where it is said of the Messiah: "On him the Spirit of the Lord will rest: a spirit of wisdom . . ." The Messiah was obviously the archetype Luke had in mind when he wrote about the seven men "full of the Spirit and of wisdom." These words bring us back to the Old Testament, where we are now going to look for instances of the hidden presence of the number 7 in the text.

Let us now have a closer look at the Isaiah passage. Utilizing our ability to count, we discover some interesting features of the text we have not noticed before: more particularly the striking structural function of the number 7.

The Hidden Presence of the Number Seven In the Old Testament

As some commentators have already observed—however, without closer investigation and without drawing any conclusions—exactly 7 qualifications have been attributed to the Spirit that rested on the Messiah. Let us number them:

> the Spirit of *the Lord* (1),
> a Spirit of *wisdom* (2) and *understanding* (3),
> a Spirit of **counsel** (4) and *power* (5),
> a Spirit of *knowledge* (6) and *fear of the Lord* (7).

What was not noticed is that the text is phrased in such a way that the word "Spirit" occurs 4 times. This could be shrugged off as mere coincidence, were it not that there are many instances in the Old Testament of the use of 4, the number expressing extensiveness (L. A. Snijders), in combination with 7, the number of abundance, wholeness and fullness, especially in the pattern $7+4 = 11$ (see chapter 4 below).

Scrutinizing the text further and registering its other features, we find that no less than three additional series of 7 emerge, which have not been noticed before, so far as I know. The first series of seven can be detected in the feats ascribed to the Messiah (verses 3–4):

> 1. his delight is in the fear of the Lord,
> 2. he does not judge by outward appearance,
> 3. he does not decide a case on hearsay,
> **4. he judges the poor with justice,**
> 5. he defends the humble in the land with equity,
> 6. his verdict strikes the ruthless like a rod,
> 7. with his word he slays the wicked.

The reason why the fourth deed has been printed in bold type is to draw attention to the fact that it appears in the mathematical center of the series, a position that gives it pride of place and therefore special emphasis—a compositional technique we discussed above in chapter 1. In light of the paramount importance of justice in the Kingdom of God and in the Messianic era, it does not surprise us that the Messiah's rule of justice receives special emphasis by its center position. This emphasis is underlined by what is said in the concluding remark (verse 5): "Righteousness shall be the girdle of his waist and faithfulness the girdle of his loins."[7]

In the next passage, verses 6–10, dealing with a description of the paradisiacal situation to be expected in the messianic era, we detect two series of 7 references to animals. The first series comprises 7 different kinds of animals:

1. the wolf, 2. the lamb, 3. the leopard
4. the kid
5. the calf, 6. the young lion, 7. the fatling (cattle).[8]

The series is concluded with the remark, "and a little child shall lead them." Verses 7–8 contain another series of 7 references to animals:

1. the cow, 2. the bear, 3. their young
4. the lion
5. the ox, 6. the cobra, 7. the viper.

The survey shows that there are no less than 4 series of 7 items hidden in the text, which suggests that the combination of 4 and 7 found in verse 2 (the 4 instances of the Spirit) is a feature in the rest of the text as well. The author of this literary gem employed the symbolic numbers 4 and 7 not only to organize the text, but especially to deepen it, imbuing it with a symbolic connotation proclaiming the fullness, completeness, and extensiveness of the Messianic era. Its fullness would extend to the four quarters of the earth!

This passage from the book of Isaiah can be considered an illustrious example demonstrating the use of counting as a compositional technique. Whoever wants to believe that what has been revealed by our investigation rests on mere coincidence, may for my part continue doing so. However, it should be realized that by turning a blind eye to the numerical aspects of the text, one not only fails to notice an essential feature of the text, but also slights the author who has produced such a beautiful work of art. A text with such features simply cannot have been written off the cuff. It was carefully composed, and in such a way that the structural numbers do not disturb the even flow of the text. We can only become aware of the presence of such numbers in a text by counting items such as key words, key phrases, stereotyped formulas, and enumeration. Let us survey some instances in the New Testament.

Examples from the Four Gospels

The number 7 regulates both genealogies of Jesus in the Gospels. According to Matt 1:1–17 there were forty-two generations from the time of Abraham to the birth of Jesus. This period of time is divided into three spans of 14 (2×7) generations, showing that the structure of Matthew's genealogy of Jesus is governed by this number. This is explicitly stated in 1:17, "There were thus 14 generations in all from Abraham to David, 14 from David to the deportation to Babylon, and 14 from the deportation until the Messiah." This structure was achieved by omitting some names in the list of the descendants of David in 1 Chronicles 3. The reason why this particular number was used to give structure to the genealogy is in the first place to imbue the text with the symbolic meaning of 14 = 2×7, the double number of fullness. Matthew obviously wanted to express what Paul called "the fullness of time" in Gal 4:4, the conviction that the time of the Messiah had fully come. But there is more to it.

Since the name of David clearly forms a pivotal point in the genealogy, it is reasonable to expect that the author would emphasize the Davidic line of descent of the Messiah. He did this by employing the numerical value of the name David (Hebrew דוד), 14 (ד=4) + (ו=6) + (ד=4) to give structure to the genealogy.[9]

The purpose of Matthew's version of the genealogy is to show that Jesus descends from Abraham through the royal line of David, not only as "son of David" but also as "son of Abraham." This is explicitly stated in the heading: "The genealogy of Jesus Christ, *son of David, son of Abraham*." Whereas Matthew used the structuring number 14 to underscore Jesus' descent from David, he employed another numerical technique in order to underline Jesus' qualification as the son of Abraham: the number 41, the numerical value of the five Hebrew letters of the name Abraham [(א=1) +(ב=2) + (ר=20) + (ה=5) + (מ=13) = 41].

In Matthew's view, there are 42 generations from Abraham to Jesus. Since Jesus was a member of the forty-second generation, there ought to be 41 progenitors. However, when I counted the names of the factual progenitors, the biological forefathers of Jesus, from Abraham through David and Jeconiah to Joseph, I found that they amount to only 40 (14 + 13 + 13), since Jeconiah's name is used twice to get 42 generations. This is rather problematic: where is the forty-first progenitor? The solution might be to add the Holy Spirit, the Spiritual Father of Jesus, between Joseph and Jesus as the forty-first "Begetter," as suggested to me by Duane Christensen in a private communication. It seems as if Matthew has intended to mention only 40 biological progenitors in order to draw attention to the missing forty-first Begetter, the Holy Spirit, upon whose role he elaborates in 1:18–25.

The genealogy of Jesus in the Gospel of Luke (chapter 3), with its 77 names, is regulated throughout by the symbolic number 7. From Jesus, son of Joseph, a genealogical line is followed back to Adam, son of God, in such a way, so it seems, that a number of important names appear in every seventh place, e.g. two Josephs, David, Abraham, Enoch, and Adam. These 11 names are: Joseph, son of Jannai (not Jesus' father, Joseph, son of Heli); Matthathias; Shealtiel; Joshua; Joseph, son of Jonam; David; Admin; Abraham; Shela; Enoch and Adam. The purpose of the Lucan genealogy is clearly to

Some Significant Numbers in the Bible

demonstrate that Jesus is "son of God" through famous ancestors such as David, Abraham, Enoch and Adam.

The number of generations from Adam to Jesus amount to 77. This significant number was chosen primarily because of its symbolical value, being the product of 7 and 11, the numbers expressing fullness and fulfillment respectively. The latent numerical message seems to be the fulfillment of the fullness of the Messianic era.

It is interesting to note, moreover, that 77 happens to represent the numerical value of the initial letters of the five Greek words Iesous, CHristos, THeou HUios, Soter, meaning "Jesus, Messiah, God's son, Savior" ($9+22+8+20+18 = 77$). These five letters together form the Greek word ICHTHUS, "Fish." As we know, the fish was an important early symbol of Christianity. It cannot be excluded that the author of this genealogy was familiar with this and that the numerical value of "fish" played a role when he chose the number 77. It is worthwhile noting that the reference to God brings the total number of names up to 78 (3×26).

Let us survey other instances of a hidden series of 7. In Luke 2:25-26 exactly 7 things are said of Simeon who witnessed the presentation of the child Jesus in the temple:

1. he was upright, 2. he was devout, 3. he waited for the restoration of Israel
4. the Holy Spirit was upon him,
5. the Holy Spirit had revealed to him, 6. that he would not see death, 7. until he had seen the Lord's Messiah.

The central position of the fourth attribute of Simeon in the text shows that his most crucial trait is that the Holy Spirit was upon him, which enabled him to pronounce his prophecy about Jesus as the Messiah.

As we have noted above, the prayer Jesus taught his followers contains seven petitions:

1. may your name be hallowed, 2. your kingdom come,
3. your will be done . . .
4. give us today our daily bread,
5. forgive us our sins . . . 6. do not put us to the test,
7. save us from evil.

A most striking feature in this prayer is that whereas the verbs in the first three petitions have the third person form, there is a change at the fourth request, which is phrased in the second person, a form that is retained throughout the rest of the prayer. The change of person gives the fourth intention of the prayer special emphasis, in the same way we noted above in Psalm 23 with regard to the words "for you are with me," where the second person appears suddenly in a third person context. Moreover, the fourth petition concerning our daily bread stands in pride of place: in the mathematical center of the series.

This petition occupies center position even in the shorter version of the prayer in the Gospel of Luke (11:2–4), which has *five* requests:

1. may your name be hallowed, 2. your kingdom come,
3. give us today our daily bread,
4. and forgive us the wrong we have done . . . 5. do not put us to the test.

What is most significant in Luke's version is that the prayer is followed by a parable in which bread and fish feature prominently (verses 5–12)! Both versions of the prayer attest to the paramount importance of food.

It goes without saying that our daily bread is of crucial importance to our very existence, in accordance with the fact that Jesus himself attached great significance to eating and drinking as witnessed by the Gospels. This is in line with the Old Testament view of the importance of vegetation as the source for sustenance: in the seven acts of creation in Genesis 1 the creation of vegetation occupies the fourth, central position (see below in chapter 4 under "The Primeval History in Genesis 1–11"). Moreover, it is underscored by the arrangement of the seven good qualities of the land of Canaan in the famous "Song of Praise for the Good Land" in Deut 8:7–10. It is a land:

1. with streams, 2. springs,
3. underground waters,
4. in which you will eat food without scarcity,
5. in which you will lack nothing,
6. whose stones are iron, and 7. in which you will mine copper.[10]

The apostle Paul was aware of the emphasizing function of the center position, for in my opinion, it is not a matter of mere coincidence that he placed hunger at the center when he wrote about the 7 things that cannot separate us from the love of Christ (Rom 8:35):

1. affliction, 2. hardship, 3. persecution,
4. hunger,
5. nakedness, 6. danger, 7. sword.

The paramount importance of bread is also stressed in the series of 7 Parables in Matthew 13, where the parable about leaven stands in central position:

1. the sower, 2. the good seed and the weeds, 3. the grain of mustard,
4. leaven,
5. the hidden treasure, 6. the merchant, 7. the net cast in sea.

To crown it all, in the series of 7 "signs" attributed to Jesus in the Gospel of John, his miraculous feeding of the crowd occupies the center position. The eighth "sign" (21:1-14) clearly stands apart, being of a different order, and may be regarded as a super additum (8=7+1). The seven coherent "signs" are:

1. changing water into wine (2:1–11);
2. healing the son of an officer (4:46–54);
3. healing the man who had been crippled for 38 years (5:1–18);
4. feeding the crowd (6:1–15—in this context Jesus refers to the "bread of life!");
5. walking on the sea (6:16–21);

6. healing a man who had been blind from birth (9:1–16);
7. raising Lazarus from the dead (11:1–46).

Let me conclude by mentioning a few more examples of conspicuous series of seven. In Matthew 5, the stereotyped formula "I say to you," used in the mouth of Jesus, occurs 7 times (verses 20, 22, 28, 32, 34, 39 and 44).[11] In Matthew 23 we find 7 woe-utterances introduced by the stereotyped phrase "Woe to you, scribes and Pharisees" (verses 13, 14, 15, 23, 25, 27 and 29).[12] The Gospel of John contains 7 "I am"-utterances by Jesus specifying his mission by means of impressive metaphors:

1. I am the bread of life (6:35);
2. I am the light of the world (8:12);
3. I am the door of the sheepfold (10:7);
4. **I am the good shepherd (10:11);**
5. I am the resurrection and the life (11:25);
6. I am the way, the truth and the life (14:6);
7. I am the true vine (15:1).

The four Gospels attribute altogether 7 utterances to Jesus on the cross, with the cry of distress, "My God, my God, why have you forsaken me?," in fourth place.

More Examples from other Books Of the New Testament

In addition to the series of 7 things Paul refers to in Romans 8, cited above, he also lists 7 gifts of the Holy Spirit (12:6–8):[13]

1. to prophecy, 2. to serve, 3. to teach,
4. **to counsel,**
5. to give generously, 6. to lead with enthusiasm, 7. to help cheerfully.

The Letter of James (3:13–18) refers to "wisdom that does not come from above" and "wisdom that comes from above." Both have 7 qualities, in accordance with the fact that the House of Wisdom has 7 pillars (Proverbs 9). The first kind is qualified as follows:

1. it is earth-bound, 2. sensual, 3. demonic;
4. **where jealousy** and
5. rivalry exist, 6. there is disorder and 7. the practice of every kind of evil.

The wisdom that comes from above, however, is:

1. pure, 2. peace-loving, 3. considerate,
4. open-minded,
5. full of mercy and good fruits, 6. impartial, 7. sincere.

The author of the Second Letter of Peter listed 7 fruits of faith belonging together as the links of a chain (1:6–7):

1. virtue, 2. knowledge, 3. self-control,
4. steadfastness,
5. piety, 6. brotherly affection, 7. love.

In addition to the numerous instances of explicit reference to 7 in the book of Revelation, of which I have given some examples above, there are a number of instances where 7 can be detected only by counting, e.g. in 5:12 where we read that the Lamb who was slain, is worthy to receive:

1. power, 2. wealth, 3. wisdom,
4. might,
5. honor, 6. glory, 7. praise.

Rev 6:15 lists 7 categories of men trying to escape from the earthquake:

1. the kings of the earth, 2. the nobles, 3. the commanders,
4. the rich,
5. the powerful, 6. all slaves, 7. all free persons.

Another list, however, in 21:8, mentions not seven but eight categories (of sinners). Like the Lamb, to whom 7 things are attributed in 5:12, as we have seen, God himself is being attributed with 7 things in 7:12 by the angels prostrating themselves before him:

1. praise, 2. glory, 3. wisdom,
4. thanksgiving,
5. honor, 6. power, 7. might.

It stands to reason that the fact that certain elements of the text appear in center position in such series, giving them pride of place, have consequences for our interpretation: we have to respect the emphasis laid on them by the authors.

The examples brought forward so far must suffice to illustrate the principle that concerns us here: the profuse use of the number 7 to give structure to the contents of the text and imbue it with a particular symbolism.

Having paid some attention to the New Testament I would now like to take the reader back to the Old Testament—a field in which I feel myself more at home—to tell how I discovered particular series of seven formulas introducing divine speeches in the Pentateuch. In so doing, I learned to count phrases, words, and verses in the Bible as a matter of course in my literary-critical analysis of the texts.

Clusters and Series of Seven Divine Speeches

The Divine Speech Formulas As an Incentive to Counting

My interest in the use of the number seven in the Old Testament gained considerable momentum when I did some research in the mid-seventies for a series of radio broadcast lectures on the idea of God speaking in the Old Testament.[1] When I scrutinized the relevant texts in the Pentateuch, I encountered a striking phenomenon: the remarkable way the biblical writers utilized the phrases introducing the so-called divine speeches, the words reported as spoken by God in the first person. Formulas or fixed forms of phrases, such as "God said," "God spoke," "the Lord said," "the Lord said to X," are used to introduce God as a character in the narrative who deliberates, communicates and speaks. Apart from such *introductory* formulas, there are phrases *referring* to God speaking such as "God had said to X," "the Lord had commanded Moses," "at the command of the Lord," "this is the command the Lord has given." The term I use to indicate both the introductory and the referring formulas is *divine speech formulas*.

What struck me in particular was the manner in which these formulas were distributed in the text of the Pentateuch in certain clusters or series. In Genesis, these concentrations occur in the creation narrative (Genesis 1), the story of Adam and

Eve (Genesis 3), the story of the flood (Genesis 6–9), and further on in Genesis chapters 15, 17, 18, 22, 31, and 35. In the book of Exodus, they are concentrated in chapters 3–4, 19, 30–31, 35, 39, and 40. And they appear in the books of Leviticus and Numbers as well. The fact that some narratives have very few or even no divine speeches at all can be explained in terms of the theological intention of the biblical authors. They could choose between using direct speech in connection with God introducing him as actively partaking in what is reported and speaking in the first person, or reporting God's activity in the third person. This would explain the clusters or concentrations of divine speeches in certain parts of the texts, but not the particular way these clusters are structured. I discovered distinct patterns, which were frequently regulated by the structural numbers 7 and 11.

Series of Seven in the Tabernacle Laws

We have known for a long time that the story of the fabrication of the desert sanctuary in Exodus 25–40 is in two distinct sections: chapters 25–31 and 35–40, interrupted by the story of the golden calf that was made by the Israelites at Mount Sinai in 32–34. A closer examination of the divine speeches in the first section, 25–31, revealed the fact that there was a significant difference in the length of the speeches.

The first speech, introduced by the formula "The Lord spoke to Moses" in 25:1, comprises the whole of 25:1 – 30:10, dealing with detailed instructions for the fabrication of the Tabernacle and its equipment. It is followed by six much shorter speeches in 30:11 – 31:17, introduced by the same stereotyped formula. Here each speech deals with one single subject. This means that there are exactly 7 divine speeches in the first section of the Tabernacle laws, Exodus 25–31.

In light of this observation, I made two conclusions. In the first place, the choice of having exactly seven speeches rests on a deliberate decision. And second, the series of seven divine speeches gives structure to the Tabernacle laws in this section and makes it into a literary unit. This insight opened my eyes to see the structuring and unifying function of this number. What I did not realize at that stage was that I would subsequently discover many more instances of this phenomenon in the Pentateuch.

Let us survey the seven divine speeches in Exodus 25–31.

1. The Lord spoke to Moses: (diverse commands)   25:1 – 30:10
2. The Lord spoke to Moses: (money for expiation)   30:11–16
3. The Lord spoke to Moses: (the bronze basin)   30:17–21
4. **The Lord spoke to Moses: (the anointing oil)**   **30:22–33**
5. The Lord spoke to Moses: (the holy spices)   30:34–38
6. The Lord spoke to Moses: (the craftsmen)   31:1–11
7. The Lord spoke to Moses: (the Sabbath)   31:12–17

What is significant here, in the first place, is the fact that the instruction for the preparation of *the holy oil-mixture* for the anointing of the Tabernacle, its equipment and the Aaronic priests, stands in the center of the series. It is not surprising to find the instruction pertaining to this extremely holy item in the center of the seven speeches, a position in which it receives special emphasis. What is more significant is that the seventh instruction deals with the keeping of the Sabbath, the seventh day of the week. This cannot be a matter of coincidence, as I would prove later when I had studied the divine speeches in Leviticus. There I discovered more instances of the link between the seventh divine speech and the Sabbath, as I shall demonstrate below.

There must be an intimate connection between the use of the number 7 to structure the divine speeches and the Sabbath. What is more, there appears to be a clear analogy between the work entrusted to Moses with regard to the Tabernacle and God's work in creating of the world. This analogy is corroborated in Exod 39:43; for after the work of the Tabernacle was completed, "Moses inspected all the work and saw that they had carried it out according to the command of the Lord, and he blessed them." God's seventh act at the time of the creation of the world was to cease work and to rest; whereas Moses' seventh assignment at the time of the fabrication of the Tabernacle is to see to the keeping of the Sabbath. As a matter of fact, the link between the keeping of the Sabbath and God's ceasing work and resting on the seventh day is explicitly stressed in the seventh divine speech: "... on the seventh day he ceased work and refreshed himself" (Exod 31:17).[2]

A closer look at the so-called second Sinai passage in Exodus 32–34, the story of Israel's apostasy, revealed that there are 13 divine speech formulas altogether introducing God's communication with Moses.[3] In the remaining chapters 35–40 there is only one introductory formula (in 40:1), bringing the total number of introductory formulas in chapters 32–40 to exactly 14 (2×7). Here again the number 7 is used to give structure and unity to the material: the series of 7 divine speech formulas in 25–31 and the series of 14 in 32–40 link the various literary units in the text of 25–40 together to form a larger unity.

My investigation of the formulas in the second section of the Tabernacle laws, the story of the carrying out of God's instructions by Moses and his assistants in Exodus 35–40, brought to light the fact that the number 7 regulates the references to God's commands given in Exod 25–31. In the story of the carrying out of God's instructions in Exod 35–38, there are 7 references to what God had earlier commanded Moses. They are not stereotyped, but phrased in various ways:

1. These are the Lord's commands to you	35:1
2. This is a thing the Lord commanded	35:4
3. Everything the Lord commanded	35:10
4. The work the Lord commanded through Moses	**35:29**
5. Exactly as the Lord commanded	36:1
6. The work the Lord commanded	36:5
7. Everything the Lord commanded Moses	38:22

The function of the number 7 symbolically representing the idea of "fullness" and "completeness" is clearly to underscore what is said in the text that *all* the tasks were executed *completely* in accordance with the instructions given by God to Moses. It should not escape our notice that, whereas the

Clusters and Series of Seven Divine Speeches 45

seventh and last divine speech in 31:12–17 deals with the keeping of the Sabbath, the passage in 35:1–3 *begins* with the Sabbath in the very first words of Moses' first address to the Israelites. Another significant feature is the special emphasis on the offerings brought by the people of Israel to the Lord for all the work of the Tabernacle: the fourth reference in 35:29 has pride of place in the center of the series.

The passage dealing with the making of the sacred vestments in 39:1–31, contains another series of 7 stereotyped formulas, with the command regarding the breastpiece in center position:

1. as the Lord commanded Moses (vestments)	39:1
2. as the Lord commanded Moses (ephod)	39:5
3. as the Lord commanded Moses (cornelians)	39:7
4. as the Lord commanded Moses (breastpiece)	**39:21**
5. as the Lord commanded Moses (ephod-mantle)	39:26
6. as the Lord commanded Moses (tunics)	39:29
7. as the Lord commanded Moses (medallion)	39:31

The following passage in Exod 39:32–43 tells how the Tabernacle with all its equipment was presented to Moses, who inspected all the work and *saw* that the craftsmen had done their work according to the command of the Lord, and he *blessed* them (verse 43). This is a clear allusion to what is said in Genesis: having performed his last act of creation, "God *saw* all he had made, and it was very good" (Gen 1:31), and in 2:3 that God rested on the seventh day, and *blessed* the day and made it holy. The analogy between Moses' *seeing* what he had accomplished and his *blessing*, on the one hand, and God's *seeing* what he had accomplished and his *blessing*, on the other, is unmistakable.

The passage in Exod 39:32–43 contains three formulas referring to God's commands. In comparison with the preceding series of seven stereotyped formulas, these three are phrased differently so as to keep the previous series of seven intact.

1. exactly as the Lord commanded Moses (all work)	39:32
2. exactly as the Lord commanded Moses (all work)	39:42
3. as the Lord commanded (all work)	39:43

The three references bring the total number of referring formulas to ten. It cannot escape our notice that this number corresponds to the number of divine utterances in Genesis 1, which we examine in greater detail below.[4]

The structure of the ten divine utterances introduced by the stereotyped formula "God said" in the Creation narrative was used by the author of the Tabernacle passage as a model to give structure to the material in Exodus 39. What we have here is yet another allusion to the analogy between the work done by Moses in regards the Tabernacle, and God's activities in creating the world. Just as God spoke ten times in getting the world and life on earth going, so Moses is said ten times to have obediently carried out God's instructions to get the Tabernacle ready and to initiate the temple-cult.[5]

This shows once again that there is a close relationship between the form of the text—including its numerical aspects—and its contents, a principle we shall illustrate later.

Let us conclude our investigation into the divine speeches in the Tabernacle laws by examining Exod 40:1–16, which includes the last of the divine speeches in Exodus where Moses is commanded to set up the Tabernacle. It is introduced by the formula "The Lord spoke to Moses," and concluded with the remark "Moses did everything exactly as the Lord had commanded him" (verse 16). The execution of God's commands by Moses is described in the next 17 verses (17–33), where 7 stereotyped formulas are used to underline *sevenfold* what has been said in verse 16:[6]

1. as the Lord commanded him (the Tabernacle)	40:19
2. as the Lord commanded him (the ark)	40:21
3. as the Lord commanded him (the table)	40:23
4. as the Lord commanded him (the lampstand)	**40:25**
5. as the Lord commanded him (the gold altar)	40:27
6. as the Lord commanded him (the screen)	40:29
7. as the Lord commanded him (the basin)	40:32

The setting up of the lampstand with its lamps occupies center position in this series of seven acts performed by Moses. The fact that its center position coincides with the fourth place in the series—which is of course a matter of contingency—reminds us of the creation of the heavenly lamps—the sun, the moon, and the stars, on the fourth day in Genesis 1. In light of various covert references to the creation narrative we have already encountered in the Tabernacle laws, our author apparently had this in mind and used it as an additional reason for putting the erection of the lampstand at this particular point in the series. The main reason, however, was to give this act pride of place in the center of the pattern of seven items.

This widely used pattern derives from the shape of the menorah, the six-branched lampstand, whose form in turn originated from the stylized tree of life, having a central stem and six branches—three on each side. The traditional term "seven-branched lampstand" is thus incorrect and should be replaced by "six-branched lampstand." The menorah is the archetype for literary compositions in which this pattern was used as a structuring device. Therefore the terms "menorah-model" and "menorah-pattern," introduced by the Austrian orientalist Claus Schedl to indicate this particular compositional pattern, are indeed appropriate.[7]

The special emphasis on the setting up of the lampstand and its lamps in the passage under discussion can only be interpreted to mean that it was regarded as having a unique significance: the installation of the symbols par excellence representing the presence of God in the sanctuary. Recent studies on the menorah have shed new light not only on its form, origin and function, but also on its symbolic significance of denoting the Presence.[8]

What is striking in our passage is the use of the phrase "for the benefit of the Lord" with regard to two specific items: the bread of the Presence (verse 23), and the lamps of the menorah (verse 25).[9] Both the bread of Presence and the lamps symbolically represent the Presence of God in the sanctuary. This conclusion is corroborated by the clear connection between the menorah and the traditions about the burning bush, the *kabod* (glory) of the Lord that filled the Tabernacle, the pillar of cloud and the pillar of fire that guided the Israelites in the desert, all of them symbolizing the Presence of the Lord.

In light of the symbolic function of the menorah in the temple, we may assume that when the biblical writers structured their texts in a menorah-pattern, they imbued them at the same time with the symbolic significance of the menorah. In other words, the menorah-patterns in the biblical text could also be meant to signify God's presence in the text. We shall discuss this in more detail in the next chapter, in connection with the divine name numbers 17 and 26 which were "woven" into the fabric of the text to "seal" it, so to speak, with God's name, which signifies his presence.

The Significance of the Menorah In Center Position

Let us return to the menorah texts in the book of Exodus to illustrate the significance of the center position of the menorah. In Exod 30:26–28, God's command to Moses to anoint the holy objects and their outfit, we count 7 items, with the menorah at the center:

1. the Tent of Meeting,
2. the Ark of the Testimony,
3. the Table and all its vessels,
4. **the Lampstand and its fittings,**
5. the Altar of Incense,
6. the Altar of Whole-offering and all its vessels,
7. the Basin and its stand.

Significantly enough this passage occurs in the fourth divine speech (30:22–33) in the center of the first series of seven divine speeches in the Tabernacle laws we have studied above. What we have here is a text with a reference to the menorah in center position right in the middle of a larger text.[10]

Clusters and Series of Seven Divine Speeches

The author of Zechariah 1–8, who was responsible for the redaction of the visions of the prophet, must have been familiar with the structure of these menorah texts. It simply cannot be a matter of coincidence that the fourth vision—that of the menorah with its lamps and the olive trees in 4:1–14—occupies center position in the semi-symmetric pattern in which the 7 visions are arranged.[11] (The texts between brackets give the chapter division we find in most translations, which is sometimes different from that in the Hebrew Bible.)

1. The horsemen and the horses	1:1–17
2. The four horns and the four smiths	2:1–4 (1:18–21)
3. The man with a measuring line	2:5ff. (2:1ff.)
4. The menorah with lamps and olive trees	**4:1–14**
5. The flying scroll	5:1–4
6. The barrel for measuring	5:5–11
7. The four chariots and their horses	6:1–8

It is worth noting that the first and last visions correspond—in the sense that both are about horses—and so form a symmetrical pattern. Another observation we can make is that the words spoken by the angel in verse 4:10b (4:4 in the Revised English Bible), which are extremely difficult to interpret, can be understood as alluding to the presence of God. The sentence, "These seven are the eyes of the Lord which range over the whole earth" can be taken as referring primarily to the stone "with seven facets" (3:9), but they can also be understood as pointing to the menorah's "seven lamps and the seven lips on each of the lamps" (4:2). In the latter case the seven lamps could be viewed as symbolically representing the seven eyes of the Lord, and, of course, the seven eyes denote God's omnipresence.

Series of Seven in the Book of Leviticus And the Sabbath

My study of the divine speeches in the book of Leviticus brought to light the same predilection for the use of the number seven to give structure to the laws that we found in the Tabernacle laws in Exodus. However, there is a significant difference between the two sets of laws. Whereas *all* instructions given to Moses regarding the building of the Tabernacle are phrased as divine speeches directed to Moses—by the use of the first person singular for God and the second person for Moses—the laws in Leviticus are characterized by the profuse use of the third person singular form in the divine speeches. Not all individual laws are introduced by separate divine speech formulas, as is the case in Exod 30:11–31:17. Some are introduced by the matter-of-fact phrase "This is the law of . . ." (see, for instance, 6:14; 7:1 and 11). This shows that the technique used in Leviticus, like that of Exodus, is to create a series of seven.

The first series of seven occurs in the sacrificial laws in Leviticus 1–6, where we find, apart from the first introductory phrase (1:1) "The Lord summoned Moses and spoke to him from the Tent of Meeting," 6 stereotyped formulas phrased "The Lord spoke to Moses." The series of seven is followed by three speeches in chapters 7–8 introduced by the same stereotyped formula. The next divine speech occurs in 10:8–11, introduced by the formula "The Lord spoke to Aaron." The narrative in 10:12–20 concludes the collection of laws in the series of eleven divine speeches in chapters 1–10, the first unmistakable instance in Leviticus of the use of the typical 7+3+1=11 (or 7+4=11) pattern.

1.	And the Lord spoke to Moses, saying	1:1
2.	And the Lord spoke to Moses, saying	4:1
3.	And the Lord spoke to Moses, saying	5:14
4.	**And the Lord spoke to Moses, saying**	**5:20 (6:1)**
5.	And the Lord spoke to Moses, saying	6:1 (6:8)
6.	And the Lord spoke to Moses, saying	6:12 (6:19)
7.	And the Lord spoke to Moses, saying	6:17 (6:24)
8.	And the Lord spoke to Moses, saying	7:22
9.	And the Lord spoke to Moses, saying	7:28
10.	And the Lord spoke to Moses, saying	8:1
11.	And the Lord spoke to *Aaron*, saying	10:8

Clusters and Series of Seven Divine Speeches 51

Before I survey the remaining divine speech formulas in Leviticus, I would draw attention to the series of seven stereotyped formulas referring to the Lord's commands to Moses in chapter 8 (reminding us of the series of seven in Exodus 39–40!).[12]

1) as the Lord commanded him	8:3
2) as the Lord commanded Moses	8:9
3) as the Lord commanded Moses	8:13
4) as the Lord commanded Moses	**8:17**
5) as the Lord commanded Moses	8:21
6) as the Lord commanded Moses	8:29
7) everything that the Lord commanded through Moses	8:36

These seven instances are followed by three differently phrased formulas in Leviticus 9–10.

1) as the Lord commanded	9:7
2) as the Lord commanded Moses	9:10
3) as the Lord commanded.	10:15

These referring formulas seem to form a 7+3=10 pattern. However, if we regard the formula in 16:34 as belonging to this series, we have the 7+4=11 pattern. Whether this is so is a matter for further study.

In Leviticus 11–16 (the purification laws) we find another series of seven stereotyped introductory formulas, "The Lord spoke to Moses (and Aaron), four of which include the name of Aaron:

1) 11:1 (+ Aaron)   2) 12:1;   3) 13:1 (+ Aaron)   4) 14:1;
5) 14:33 (+ Aaron)   6) 15:1 (+ Aaron)   7) 16:1.

An additional formula, occurring in 16:2, is phrased differently: "The Lord said to Moses," in order not to disturb the series of seven, a technique we have encountered above, and which we shall confront again.

The so-called Holiness Code in Leviticus 17–26 seems to have two series of seven stereotyped introductory formulas, phrased "The Lord spoke to Moses." This view of the series depends on the supposition that the two divine speeches in chapters 17–18 should be regarded as an introduction to the collection of laws in 19–26, where the term "Be holy, for I, the Lord your God, am holy" occurs for the first time in chapter 19. The eighth formula (in 21:1) is phrased "The Lord said to Moses," once again, as we have seen, to keep the series of seven stereotyped formulas in Lev 19–23 intact.[13]

1) The Lord spoke to Moses	19:1
2) The Lord spoke to Moses	20:1
3) The Lord spoke to Moses	21:16
4) The Lord spoke to Moses	**22:1**
5) The Lord spoke to Moses	22:17
6) The Lord spoke to Moses	22:26
7) The Lord said to Moses	23:1

This series is concluded in 23:8 by an instruction with regard to "the seventh day," which brings to mind what we have seen in the first series of 7 divine speeches in the Tabernacle laws, where the concluding speech deals with the Sabbath (Exod 31:12–17).

The introductory formulas to the divine speeches in the second series of 7 in the Holiness laws are formulated in the same stereotyped manner, except that the seventh is longer: "The Lord spoke to Moses on Mount Sinai."

1) The Lord spoke to Moses	23:9
2) The Lord spoke to Moses	23:23
3) The Lord spoke to Moses	23:26
4) The Lord spoke to Moses	**23:33**
5) The Lord spoke to Moses	24:1
6) The Lord spoke to Moses	24:13
7) The Lord spoke to Moses on Mount Sinai	25:1

The divine speech at the center of the series is about the 7-day Feast of Booths in the seventh month. The seventh speech deals mainly with the Sabbath Years and the Year of Jubilee, the quintessence of the Sabbath!

The first results of my investigation into the use of divine speech formulas in the Old Testament supplied the definitive proof in my mind that the number seven played an important role as a structuring device in the two large so-called priestly passages in the books of Exodus and Leviticus. Some of the results of my investigation were published in 1978.[14]

I was convinced not only that I had detected a significant aspect of the biblical text, but also that there must be more to be discovered regarding the use of the divine speech formulas in the Pentateuch. This supposition was shown to be true in further research on the subject. From the start, the phenomenon intrigued me and aroused my curiosity. In my leisure time, I began to mark the introductory and referring formulas in the Pentateuch with highlighters of different colors to make them visible. What I gradually found made me realize that the use of these formulas, which had not been studied systematically before, needed to be investigated more thoroughly.

More Examples of Manifestly Designed Series of Seven Items

The opportunity to explore the matter more deeply presented itself in the fall of 1981, when I sprained my ankle playing volleyball and had to take some rest. Making a virtue of the necessity, I sat at my desk to register the divine speech formulas in the Pentateuch. Much to my delight, I found that clusters or series of divine speech formulas were not limited to the so-called priestly passages. They occurred throughout the books of Genesis–Numbers, for instance:

- the cluster of ten stereotyped introductory formulas in Gen 1:3, 6, 9, 11, 14, 20, 24, 26, 28, 29 in the pattern $7+3=10$, to which we shall return below;
- the cluster of seven in Gen 3:9, 11, 13, 14, 16, 17, 22;
- the series of ten in 6–9 (6:3, 7, 13; 7:1, 15, 21; 9:1; 9:8, 12, 17) in a $7+3=10$ pattern;
- the series of eleven in 31–32 (31:3, 11, 12, 24, 29; 32:10, 13, 27, 28, 29, 30)—$7+4=11$ pattern;
- the series of seven in 35–48 (35:1, 10, 11; 46:2a, 2b, 3; 48:4);
- the cluster of seven in Gen 15:1–16 (1, 4, 5a, 5b, 7, 9, 13);
- the cluster of seven in Exod 4:1–17 (2, 3, 4, 6, 7, 11, 14).

A closer examination of the two latter instances showed the unmistakable aim of the author to achieve exactly seven introductory formulas.

In Gen 15:1–16, the conversation between God and Abram, there appears to be a formula (in 5b) that does not seem to be strictly necessary, since it occurs directly after the preceding divine speech in verse 5a. The text is structured as follows:

1. The *word of the Lord* came to Abram (verse 1); and Abram's response (verses 2–3);
2. The *word of the Lord* came to him (verse 4);
3. He brought Abram outside and *said* (verse 5a);
4. **Then He said to him (verse 5b);**[15] **and Abram's response (verse 6);**
5. And He *said* to him (verse 7); and Abram's response (verse 8);
6. And He *said* to him (verse 9); and Abram's response (verses 10–12);
7. And He *said* to Abram (verse 13).

In the next passage, Gen 15:17–21, the author used a different formula (verse 18) to introduce God's covenant with Abram, in order not to disturb this manifestly designed seven instances of introductory formulas. Instead of using the finite verb, he chose the infinitive form: "That day the Lord made a covenant with Abram, saying."[16]

The extra divine speech formula does not disturb the even course of the text when we read it, because it has a clear function in the context: to give Abram the time to look at the stars before God resumes and speaks about Abram's descendants. This observation confirms what we have noticed already: the ingenious way in which the text has been composed so that the numerical aspects do not upset the smooth course of the narrative.

Let us now examine the second passage, Exod 4:1–17—the narrative about God's instructing Moses to prepare him for his mission—as an example of a text with a cluster of seven formulas in which we miss obviously indispensable introductory formulas. Since the lacking of formulas in a text is more conspicuous than extra ones, an attentive reader will easily locate the spots where we miss introductory formulas. The passage is structured as follows:

1. *The Lord said to him*: "What is that in your hand?" (2a); Moses' response (2b);

2. *And He said*: "Cast it on the ground!" (3a); Moses' reaction (3b);

3. *But the lord said to Moses*: "*Put out your hand and take it by the tail!*"—so he put out his hand and caught it and it became a rod in his hand—
   "*that they may believe that the Lord, the God of their fathers, the God of Abraham, the God of Isaac, and the God of Jacob has appeared to you.*" (4–5);

4. *Then the Lord said to him*: "Put your hand into your bosom!" (6a);
   Moses obeys and his hand was leprous (6b);

5. *And He said*: "*Put your hand back into your bosom!*"—and when he took it out, behold, it was as healthy as the rest of his body—"*If they will not believe you, or heed the first sign, they may believe the latter sign. If they will not believe even these two signs, or heed your voice, you shall take some water from the Nile and pour it upon the ground . . .*" (7–9);
   Moses responds, stating his objections (10);

6. *Then the Lord said to him*: (God's response: 11–12); Moses' answer (13);

7. Then the Lord became angry with Moses *and he said*: (God commands Moses to go and accomplish his mission: 14–17).

In the third and the fifth divine speeches, the author interrupted God's words with the narrative and let God continue to speak without using an introductory phrase—in verse 5 and verse 8, where we would expect a new introductory formula. Moreover, God's instruction to Moses to perform a third miracle is not introduced by a separate introductory phrase, but is incorporated in the fifth speech. All this illustrates the author's intention to obtain 7 introductory formulas.

In chapter 5 we shall have a still closer look at this brilliantly composed text which has a number of other fascinating numerical aspects, one of which is that the total number of (Hebrew) words used in the introductory formulas adds up to 17, the extremely holy number representing the name YHWH. The author's obvious intention to obtain this number explains the great variety in length of the introductory formulas: 1) 3 words; 2) 1 word; 3) 4 words; 4) 4 words; 5) 1 word; 6) 3 words; 7) 1 word.

Let us now examine a pattern we have already touched upon: the 7+4=11 pattern, a structuring principle of which I have discovered numerous instances particularly in Genesis and in Deuteronomy.

The 7+4=11 Pattern in the Pentateuch

The Primeval History in Genesis 1–11

In the survey given above we came across an example of the 7+4=11 pattern in the series of eleven introductory formulas in Genesis 31–32 (31:3, 11, 12, 24, 29; 32:10, 13, 27, 28, 29, 30). I have also drawn attention to the ten stereotyped introductory formulas in Genesis 1 and in 6–9, where I referred to a 7+3=10 pattern. However, a more attentive study of the context revealed that the latter pattern, which is there all the same, is really the major part of the longer, more frequently occurring 7+3+1=11 or 7+4=11 pattern.

I became aware of the existence of this pattern when I surveyed and charted the divine speech formulas in the whole of the so-called Primeval History, Genesis 1–11. There appeared to be no less than six instances of this pattern in these eleven chapters: three in the structure of the divine speech formulas, and three in the genealogies in Genesis 4, 5 and 10. Let us examine those pertaining to the divine speeches first.

The Primeval History can be divided into three distinct parts:

a) the *Story of Creation* in Gen 1:1 – 2:3;
b) the *Story of Adam and Eve* in Gen 2:4 – 4:26;
c) the *Story of Humanity* in Genesis 5–11, including the Story of the Flood in 6–9.

The chart I made of the introductory divine speech formulas convinced me that they not only give structure to the material, but they also tie the diverse elements together to give them unity. Let me illustrate what I mean, starting with the eleven divine speeches pertaining to creation, which can be divided into three categories.

    a) heaven and earth with all their living creatures
    b) humanity
    c) womankind

a) The creation of the cosmos and all its living creatures
    1. And God said: *command regarding light*   1:3
    2. And God said: *command regarding the firmament*   1:6
    3. And God said: *command regarding the sea and earth*   1:9
    4. And God said: command regarding vegetation   **1:11**
    5. And God said: *command regarding heavenly bodies*   1:14
    6. And God said: *command regarding creatures/birds*   1:20
    7. And God said: *command regarding cattle/beasts*   1:24[1]

b) The creation of humanity
    8. And God said: *deliberation to create human beings*   1:26
    9. And God said: *blessing for human beings*   1:28
    10. And God said: *providing food for human beings*   1:29[2]

c) The creation of womankind
    11. And the Lord God said: *decision to create Eve*   2:18

The author clearly wanted to attain the pattern he intended: $7+3+1=11$.

In Genesis 1–2, two additional divine speeches are cited: the blessing of the living creatures and birds in 1:22 and the command regarding the trees in the garden in 2:16. Both of them clearly fall outside the series of eleven utterances introduced by stereotyped formulas using the finite verb "to say." God's blessing in 1:22 is simply introduced by the words "And God blessed them, saying," without the use of the finite verb "he said." Likewise God's command in 2:16 is introduced by the phrase "And God commanded the man, saying."

On the other hand, however, the blessing for mankind in 1:28, being on a higher level than the low-key blessing in 1:22, is introduced by the crucial stereotyped formula "and God said" used throughout the series.[3] The seven divine utterances in category a) are clearly commands, distinguishing them from those in categories b) and c), which have quite a different character, being divine deliberations or decisions expressing God's thoughts (numbers 8 and 11), and divine addresses expressing his blessing of mankind and his measures regarding food (numbers 9 and 10). This means that not only formally but also as regards contents the first seven utterances belong together. This string of seven divine utterances in Gen 1:1–25 is inextricably linked to the next three utterances in 1:26–30.

In the first of these, in 1:26, God does not create through his commanding word, but deliberates and reflects on his plan to create human beings. God's thoughts are expressed in words in the form of a soliloquy or interior monologue. In the second utterance, in 1:28, God is presented as giving his blessing to mankind, addressing them directly. Finally, in the third, God expresses the measures he has taken to provide food for mankind and all other creatures.

The way in which the author speaks about the creation of mankind as an act that does not fit into the previous seven acts of creation, shows that it was considered to belong to a different category, being on a higher level. Therefore it is presented as the result of a separate and special act of divine deliberation and reflection. This observation shows once again how the form and structure of a text can give us information about its contents. Strictly speaking, there are not ten "words of creation"—an often used, but incorrect term—but seven. However, these seven utterances and the following three belong both structurally and with respect to contents inseparably together in a fixed pattern: $7+3=10$.

This coherence is found also in the eleventh divine utterance in 2:18—God's decision to create Eve; for it is a deliberation just like that in 1:26 regarding the creation of human beings. From the perspective of creation, God's decision to create Eve cannot be separated from the preceding acts of creation. The chain of creative acts that runs through Genesis 1 does not cease before it comes to an end in Gen 2:18. God's creation attains its completion only in the creation of "the mother of all living beings" (3:20).

From a literary point of view, the story about the creation of Eve does not actually belong to the Story of Creation, since it is part of the Story of Adam and Eve in Gen 2:4 – 4:26. This is also attested by the use of the divine designation "The Lord God" in the introductory formula in 2:18, which is the name that is currently used in this story. However, the Story of Creation and the Story of Adam and Eve were composed as inseparably connected links of the narrative chain that stretches from the creation of the world to the Babylonian Exile, and were intended to be read as one continuous story.[4]

What we have said about the creation of mankind on the basis of a special divine deliberation applies *mutatis mutandis* to the creation of Eve, as a "partner suited to him"—not "helper to fit him"—who represents *woman*kind, as Adam represents *man*kind. In light of this, the creation of the female human being is thus placed on a different, and incontestably higher level than the creation of the male. This is also expressed by the idea that she was created uniquely from a rib of the male, who was considered to have been "formed of dust from the ground" (2:7).

Let us now survey and chart the divine speech formulas in the rest of the Story of Adam and Eve (Genesis 3–4). It will show that the 7+4=11 pattern was used here too, linking the Story of the Fall (Genesis 3) with that of Cain and Abel (Genesis 4). In chapter 3, we find three references to a divine saying, which fall outside the series of introductory formulas:

- in 3:1 the snake cites God's command: "*Did God not say*, 'You shall not eat of any tree of the garden?'"
- in 3:3 the woman refers to God's command: ". . . *but God said*, 'You shall not eat of the fruit of the tree which is in the middle of the garden . . .'"
- in 3:17 God refers to what he had commanded: ". . . the tree of which I *commanded you, saying*: 'You shall not eat of it . . .'"

There are eleven formulas introducing the divine speeches in the discourse between God and the other characters in the story.

1.	The Lord God *called* to the man and said to him	3:9
2.	And he said	3:11
3.	And the Lord said to the woman	3:13
4.	**And the Lord God said to the snake**	**3:14**
5.	To the woman he said	3:16
6.	To the man he said	3:17
7.	Then the Lord God said (deliberation)	3:22
8.	And the Lord said to Cain	4:6
9.	And the Lord said to Cain	4:9
10.	And he said	4:10
11.	And the Lord said to him	4:15

The series of eleven introductory formulas begin with God's *calling* to man, which is in fact calling him to account. This not only concerns Adam and Eve but also Cain. A closer examination of the use of the verb "to call" with God as subject brings some interesting facts to light. First, it occurs exactly seven times in the Primeval History (1:5a, 5b, 8, 10a, 10b; 3:9; 5:2). Second, in 5:2 the verb seems to open the series of eleven divine speeches in chapters 6–11 (see further below). Third, it appears to have the same function at the beginning of the series of divine speeches in Exod 3:4 onwards; Exod 19:3 onwards; Exod 24:16 onwards and in Lev 1:1 onwards, which I will not discuss further in detail here.[5]

There are no divine speeches in Genesis 5. The only reference to God's speaking is what is said in verse 2: "He created the male and female and he blessed them and *called* them man." By the way, this is the seventh and last occurrence of the verb "to call" with God as subject in the Primeval History. In the Story of the Flood, Genesis 6–9, I have detected a series of seven divine utterances from the beginning up to God's blessing of Noah and his sons after the flood (6:3 – 9:7). This series is followed by three divine speeches dealing with God's covenant with Noah and his offspring, in 9:8–17. In the rest of the Primeval History, there occurs only one divine speech: in the

Story of the Tower of Babel in Gen 11:6–7. The 7+3+1=11 pattern speaks for itself in the following survey:

1. And the Lord said (*deliberation*) — 6:3
2. And the Lord said (*deliberation*) — 6:7
3. And God said to Noah (command to build the ark) — 6:13
4. **And the Lord said to Noah (command to enter it)** — **7:1**
5. And the Lord spoke to Noah (command to leave it) — 8:15
6. And the Lord said in his heart (*deliberation*) — 8:21
7. And God blessed Noah and his sons and said to them — 9:1

8. Then God said to Noah and his sons (covenant) — 9:8
9. And God said (about the sign of the covenant) — 9:12
10. And God said to Noah (once again about the sign) — 9:17
11. And the Lord said (*deliberation*) — 11:6

There is a close correspondence between the 7+3=10 pattern here in Gen 6:3 – 9:7 and that in Genesis 1, which must have been used as an archetype. Moreover, in my mind there is no doubt at all that the 7+3+1=11 pattern we detected in Genesis 1–2, and in Genesis 3–4, was copied here to give structure to the whole text of Genesis 6–11.

The remarkable, obviously redundant introductory formulas in 9:12 and 17, in the middle of God's address to Noah and his sons, shows that the author took pains to achieve ten formulas. This observation underscores what we have said above in connection with the extra, apparently redundant, introductory formula in Gen 15:5b—that it served to achieve a specific number of formulas, seven in that case. Of course, the "redundant" formulas have a distinct literary function: to mark the change of perspective in the divine speech.

The Eleven Divine Monologues In the Pentateuch

There are eleven instances in the Pentateuch in which God is presented as talking to himself. These private divine deliberations have the form of soliloquies, also called interior monologues, in which God expresses his thoughts, intentions, and decisions: he "speaks in his heart" (Gen 8:21). It appears that this particular form of God's speaking is used in the Pentateuch, and probably elsewhere, when it concerns crucial matters. In such cardinal matters, God does not act spontaneously, but ponders and reflects before making a decision.[6] We have already encountered seven of these monologues in the Primeval History. However, there are three more in the Tetrateuch—one in Genesis 18 and two in the book of Exodus (chapters 3 and 13)—and one in Deuteronomy 32, bringing the total to eleven. The numbers at the end of the lines give the amount of words in the introductory formulas and in the speeches respectively.

1. Decision to create human beings (1:26)   2 + 17
2. Decision to create Eve (2:18)   3 + 9/26
3. Decision to banish Adam and Eve (3:22)   3 + 19
4. **Decision to limit human life span (6:3)**   **2 + 13**
5. Decision to wipe out the human race (6:7)   2 + 20
6. Decision to spare the earth (8:21–22)   4 + 23
7. Decision to confuse Babel's language (11:6–7)   2 + 28

8. Decision to inform Abraham (18:17–19)   2 + 42
9. Decision to lead Israel from Egypt (Exod 3:17)   1 + 17
10. Decision to alter Israel's route (Exod 13:17)   3 + 7
11. Decision to hide his face (Deut 32:20–27)[7]   2 + 94

             Total number of words: 26 + 289
             $289 = 17 \times 17$!

It should be noted that the limitation of the human life span occupies fourth place, at the center of the seven monologues in the Primeval History, the dispersion of the human race over the face of the earth being in seventh place.

Hans Nobel has studied the divine monologues particularly with regard to their numerical aspects in his dissertation on the eleven divine thoughts in Genesis–2 Kings.[8] In this meticulous study, he criticizes my view that there are eleven monologues in the Pentateuch and insists that Exod 13:17 should not be considered a monologue. In his view, Judg 2:20–22, God's decision not to help Israel drive out the other nations from Canaan but to test Israel through them, is the eleventh instance. Without going into the arguments for maintaining my own position, I would call attention to the fact that my view is underscored by an important numerical consideration. The two divine name numbers 17 and 26 significantly govern the eleven monologues in the Pentateuch. The total number of words in the introductory formulas amounts to 26, while there are exactly 289 (17×17) words in the monologues themselves. Can this be mere coincidence?[9]

The examples given above must suffice to illustrate the numerical patterns of 7 and 7+3+1=11 in the structure of the divine speeches in the Pentateuch.[10] The numerical aspects of the divine speeches are not limited, however, to the use of the structuring numbers 7 and 11. On the contrary, there is much more to these speeches, as we shall see in the next chapter. We have not finished with them yet. As a matter of fact, it was the study of the divine addresses that opened my eyes to the function of the numbers 17 and 26 and to their exceedingly high frequency of occurrence in these speeches.

Before we address this fascinating issue, let me conclude the present chapter by giving some examples of the use of the 7+4=11 pattern outside the divine speeches.

Three Genealogies in Genesis 1–11

I detected this pattern also in three genealogies in Genesis 1–11 and in the so-called *toledoth*-formulas, "this is the history/offspring of . . ." occurring eleven times in Genesis.

Let us examine the three genealogies first, namely the lineage:

    I.   from **Adam** to the offspring of Lamech in Gen 4:1–22
   II. from **Adam** to the offspring of Noah in Gen 5:1–32
  III. from **Shem** to the offspring of Terah in Gen 11:10–27

	I—Gen 4:1–22	II—Gen 5:1–32	III—Gen 11:10–27
1	Adam	Adam	Shem
2	Cain	Seth	Arpaxad
3	Enoch	Enosh	Shelah
4	Irad	Kenan	Eber
5	Mehujael	Mahalalel	Peleg
6	Methushael	Jared	Reu
7	**Lamech**	**Enoch**	**Serug**
8	Jabal	Methuselah	Nahor
9	Jubal	Lamech	Terah
10	Tubal-Cain	Noah	Abram/Nahor/Haran
11	Naamah	Shem/Ham/Japhet	Lot

I would make two observations: first, in the genealogy of Adam via Seth, the *three sons* of Noah represent one generation, which also goes for the *three sons* of Terah in the genealogy of Shem. The *three sons* of Lamech, however, in the genealogy of Adam via Cain, represent three different social groups and should therefore be listed separately. Second, it is significant to notice that the seventh descendant in the first genealogy of Adam, Lamech, is not simply listed like his predecessors without further ado, but appears to receive special attention by the author, who tells something more about him. The prominence of Lamech is stressed not only by this but also by the fact that he occupies the seventh place. Significantly enough, the same is true for Enoch in the second genealogy of Adam, emphasizing his prominence as well. This pattern suggests that the person in seventh position in the genealogy of Shem, Serug, has also been endowed with a special status. What seems to be significant about him is that he concludes the line of Shem's descendants *before* the emergence of the Abraham-group, starting with Abraham's grandfather Nahor. Lot, the son of Haran, owes his mention in the genealogy to the fact that he plays a specific role in the history of Abraham.[11]

The Eleven *Toledoth*-Formulas in Genesis

The words ʾ*elleh toledoth*, literally "these are the begettings/procreations of . . ." should be translated either: "these are the descendants of . . ." or "this is the (hi)story/offspring of . . ." or "this is the (hi)story of the descendants of . . ." Since a genealogy itself was regarded as "history," it is difficult to decide which rendering to choose in each instance, but since it is not relevant in the present context, I shall translate consistently "this is the history of . . ." without implying of course that they deal with history in the modern sense of the word.

1.	This is the history of heaven and earth	2:4
2.	This is the history of Adam	5:1
3.	This is the history of Noah	6:9
4.	**This is the history of Noah's sons**	**10:1**
1/5.	This is the history of Shem	11:10
2/6.	This is the history of Terah (Abraham!)	11:27
3/7.	This is the history of Ishmael	25:12
4/1.	**This is the history of Isaac (Jacob and Esau!)**	**25:19**
5/2.	This is the history of Esau	36:1
6/3.	This is the history of Esau, father of Edom	36:9
7/4.	This is the history of Jacob (Joseph!)[12]	37:2

The survey shows that the book of Genesis is structured by these eleven "headings" phrased with the stereotyped formula ʾ*elleh toledoth*, introducing eleven narrative blocks. At first glance, the familiar 7+4=11 pattern seems to occur here in reverse order: 4+7=11—that is, if we take the flood as a turning point, which seems to be the most important caesura in the Genesis narrative. It is still possible, however, that the current order of 7+4=11 was intended. In that case the turning point is the death of Abraham (Gen 25:1–11) and the "history of Ishmael" in Gen 25:12–18, which concludes the Abraham cycle (Gen 11:27 – 25:11). After this caesura, we find the story of Jacob and Esau, introduced in 25:19 by the formula, "this is the history of Isaac."

The Role of 7 in the Life Spans Of the Patriarchs

In passing, I would call attention to the function of 7 in the rather baffling exceptionally high life spans attributed to the antediluvian ancestors of humanity in Genesis 5. In light of Gen 6:3, where it is said that God limited the life span of humans to 120 years, it is clear that the high life spans here, and in the genealogy of Shem in Gen 11:10–32, and those mentioned elsewhere, should not be taken in a fundamentalistic/rationalistic way as real historical data. These numbers were intended to be symbolic, whether or not we are able to recover their precise meaning.

The Austrian orientalist and biblical scholar Claus Schedl has suggested a plausible explanation for the life spans of five of the ten antediluvian patriarchs: Mahalalel (895 years), Jared (962 years), Enoch (365 years), Methuselah (969 years) and Lamech (777 years). The life span of 365 years, the number of days in a solar year, attributed to Enoch suggests a connection with the planets. According to Schedl, who refers to the calculations of the French scholar M. Barnouin, the life spans of the four others should be interpreted as representing the orbital times (in days) of two planets in conjunction:[13]

Mercury + Mars	116 + 780 = 896(5)	Mahalalel
Venus + Saturn	584 + 378 = 962	Jared
Jupiter + Saturn	399 + 378 = 777	Lamech.

The highest life span of all, the 969 years of Methuselah, is interpreted by Schedl as 840 (7×120) plus the sum of the digits in the years mentioned with respect to these three: their age at the begetting of a successor, the rest of their years, and their total life span:

	Begetting-age	Remaining Years	Total life span	Sum of digits
Mahalalel	65	830	895	44
Jared	162	800	862	34
Lamech	182	595	777	51

Methuselah's life span can be explained as 129 (= 44 + 34 + 51) = + 840 = 969. A comparable procedure is used in regards the life span of Joseph, whose 110 years are made up of the sum of numbers featuring in the life spans of his predecessors—see chapter 5 under "The Divine Name Numbers Signifying God's Presence."

K. Th. Eisses has drawn attention to the fact that the sum of the begetting ages of all ten patriarchs (1556) and the sum of their remaining years (7019) have special significance: the sum of their digits is 17. He presents several rather complicated calculations to show that there are more instances of the presence of the numbers 17 and 26 in this genealogy. See his article cited in note 13.

The life spans of the five remaining patriarchs have not yet been explained satisfactorily—that of Adam, Seth, Enosh, Kenan, and Noah. Schedl's interpretation of the life span of Methuselah, taking 840 as the basic number to which another number has been added, could provide the key to solve the riddle of the remaining life spans. The number 840 should be interpreted as representing a supermaximum life span: 7 times the maximum of 120 years according to Gen 6:3. Could these five life spans have been constructed by the addition of particular numbers to the supermaximum of 840 years? If we deduct 840 from the life spans attributed to the remaining patriarchs, we get five reasonable, normal life spans.

Adam	930 - 840 = 90 years
Seth	912 - 840 = 72 years
Enosh	905 - 840 = 65 years
Kenan	910 - 840 = 70 years
Noah	950 - 840 = 110 years

How these numbers should be interpreted is not certain, but I would suggest that they might have had a particular function in connection with the ways of dividing the time span between Creation and the flood into periods. As I cannot go into this fascinating material here any further, it must suffice to refer to the literature on the subject.[14]

There is no evidence to support the idea that the symbolic number 7 played a role in the life spans of the patriarchs Abraham (175), Isaac (180), Jacob (147), and Joseph (110), and the matriarch Sarah (127). The suggestion that Sarah's 127 years = $2 \times 60 + 7$, Isaac's 180 years = 3×60, and Jacob's 147 years = $2 \times 70 + 7$, is too facile to be taken seriously. Moreover, it does not explain the life spans of Abraham and Joseph. We shall return later to the life span of Sarah. I have discovered that the life spans of these four patriarchs have nothing to do with the number 7, since they were derived schematically from the divine number 17, as shown in the next chapter.[15]

How Did 7 Acquire Its Symbolic Meaning?

The extreme popularity of the number 7 as a structuring device in the Bible calls for an explanation of its symbolic significance expressing fullness, completeness, abundance, and the maximum, the highest possible attainable amount or number. In the previous chapter, we have referred to this number when we studied the origin of the symbolism of closely related number 12, signifying completeness, perfection, and totality. Both numbers derive their symbolic meaning from the combination of 3 and 4, 12 being the product of these factors and 7 their sum.

As we have seen, 3 represents the three vertical dimensions of the cosmos: the vault of heaven, the earth and the nether world, and 4 the horizontal dimensions: the four quarters. Thus 12 was used particularly to express the idea of the perfect, harmonious totality, while 7 was employed to signify more specifically the cosmic totality, being the sum of 3, representing the heavenly totality, and 4 representing the terrestrial totality. This made 7 an extremely holy number, not only in ancient Israel but also in Egypt, Mesopotamia and among other peoples in the ancient Near East and elsewhere in the world.[16]

In Israel, the popularity of 7 as a structuring device was considerably enhanced by its use in the Story of Creation and, as we have shown above, by imitating the shape of the Menorah, with its unmistakable focal point flanked by six branches. The belief in antiquity that there were seven planets certainly contributed to the popularity of 7, linking it once again with the heavens. In addition to this, 7 played a crucial role in time reckoning and in fixing religious festivals. The lunar month of 28 days consisted of 4 cycles of 7 days, determined by the 4 phases of the moon.

The combination of 4 and 7 brings us to the symbolism of their sum, 11, the less known but nevertheless important symbolic number, which we have already encountered in Luke's genealogy of Jesus.

The Number of Fulfillment, 11

The number eleven, the sum of 4 as the number of extensiveness and 7 as the number of fullness seems to have developed in the course of time a separate status and its own characteristic symbolism. The fact that we have encountered the number 11 several times and in diverse respects in the Primeval History in the first eleven chapters of Genesis, could be an indication of its symbolic function: to express the idea of fulfillment. The divine blessing in Gen 1:28 explicitly encourages male and female human beings to be fruitful and increase, "and to fill the earth." Significantly enough verse 28 is composed of exactly 22 (2×11) words and 88 (8×11) letters (in the Hebrew text). That there are 11 chapters in the Primeval History according to the chapter division we have in our translations may be a matter of coincidence, but it cannot be excluded that this division was partly based upon knowledge of the use of the number 11 in Genesis.

This goes for the first eleven chapters of Deuteronomy too. When I wrote my commentary on Deuteronomy 1–11, I found several instances of the use of the 7+4=11 pattern giving structure to the "larger" and "smaller" literary units.[17]

A glance at the table of contents will give the reader an impression of the use of the pattern in the structure of the eleven "larger literary units" in chapters 1–3 and the seven "larger literary units" in chapters 4–11. In the survey on the following page, the "larger units" are printed bold and numbered I, II, etc.; the "smaller units" are numbered 1, 2, etc.

We shall examine more closely the intriguing menorah-structure of Deuteronomy 4–11 in chapter 5—and its fascinating central chapter 7 having its own menorah-structure—see under the heading "Counting Verses in Deuteronomy." It must suffice here to say that not only the "larger literary units" 4:1–43 and 5:1 – 6:3 but also 10:12 – 11:32 are structured by the 7+4=11 pattern, and that the two passages that flank the central chapter, 6:4–25 and 8:1 – 9:6, together form the pattern 4+7=11.[19]

In the first eleven chapters of Genesis, we find the story of the increase and expansion of the human race over the face of the earth and the development of different nations. It is therefore not surprising to see how the three genealogies are structured by the 7+4=11 pattern. Neither did it surprise me when I examined Gen 11:1–9, the Story of the Tower of Babel, and discovered that the passage consists of exactly 121 (11×11) words, and found that verse 8, telling how God dispersed the people from there all over the earth, comprises 11 words.

One could shrug all this off as a matter of pure chance, but there is more evidence of the use of the number 11 in passages dealing with the idea of fulfillment and filling. One of the aims of the stories in Genesis 12–50 about the wanderings of the landless patriarchs is to give substance to the belief that God promised to increase their numbers and to give them land to settle. As we know, the books of Exodus through Joshua tell the story of the fulfillment of these promises: how

Deuteronomy 1–3 + 4:44–49[18]

I	1:1–5	Preface introducing the whole book
II	1:6–18	Horeb, starting point for the journey
		1. 1:6–8
		2. 1:9–15
		3. 1:16–18.
III	1:19 – 2:1	From Kadesh to the promised land
		4. 1:19–22
		5. 1:23–28
		6. 1:29–33
		7. 1:34–40
		8. 1:41–45
		9. 1:46 – 2:1.
IV	2:2–15	From Seir to the Zared
		10. 2:2–8a
		11. 2:8b-15;
V	2:16–25	Crossing the Arnon
		12. 2:16–19
		13. 2:20–23
		14. 2:24–25.
VI	2:26–37	Conquest of the land of Sihon
		15. 2:26–30
		16. 2:31–35
		17. 2:36–37.
VII	3:1–10	Conquest of the land of Og
		18. 3:1–4
		19. 3:5–7
		20. 3:8–10.
VIII	3:11–17	Occupation of the conquered land
		21. 3:11–14
		22. 3:15–17.
IX	3:18–22	Moses commands the conquest of Canaan
		23. 3:18–20
		24. 3:21–22.
X	3:23–29	Entrance refused to Moses
		25. 3:23–25
		26. 3:26–29.
XI	4:44–49	Epilogue

the Israelites increased and ultimately settled in Canaan and "filled" the promised land.

My interpretation of the symbolic significance of 11 as the number expressing fulfillment was convincingly underscored by the results of my study of the numerical aspects of Deuteronomy 1–3. These chapters deal with preparations to continue the journey form Horeb to Canaan and the initial fulfillment of the promise of land to the patriarchs and their descendants: the Edomites, Moabites, Ammonites, and Israelites. What I discovered astounded me. I found a unique and unprecedented accumulation of the number 11 and its multiples, which I encountered nowhere else. The following survey shows the number of words in these passages:

1:19–22	The promised land in sight	77 (7×11)
2:2–6	God's speech: **land for Esau/Edom**	55 (5×11)
2:7	Moses' address	22 (2×11)
2:9–13b	God's speech: **land for Lot/Moab**	66 (6×11)
2:18–25	God's speech: **land for Lot/Ammon**	121 (11×11)
2:16 – 3:29	Total number of words	770 (70×11)
3:2	God's speech: **land for Israel**	22 (2×11)
3:1–7	Narrative: the march to Bashan	110 (10X11)
3:18–20	Quotation by Moses	55 (5×11)
3:23–29	Moses' request to enter the land	99 (9×11)
3:26–28	God's speech: **no land for Moses**	44 (4×11)

A significant detail is that the 110 words in 3:1–7 are evenly divided: 55 in the main clauses and 55 in the subordinate clauses; the 99 words in 3:23–29 are likewise divided into 55 + 44.

These data can be checked in the appendix to my commentary, volume IA, where the reader will find a transcription of the Hebrew text and the numerical structural analysis of 1–11.

It would be worthwhile to carry out a more comprehensive investigation into the use of this almost forgotten intriguing number, which has not yet received the attention it deserves. But let us now address a still more fascinating numerical aspect of the biblical texts: the use of the numbers 17 and 26.

5

The Secret of the Hidden Sacred Numbers 17 and 26

Significant Numbers
In the Divine Speeches in Genesis

The logical follow-up of my inventory of the introductory and referring divine speech formulas in the Pentateuch was an investigation into the numerical aspects of the divine speeches themselves. Since I was particularly intrigued by the divine monologues at that time, I started with the divine deliberations in the Primeval History and counted the words both in the introductory formulas and in the eleven speeches. See the table in chapter 4 under "The Eleven Divine Monologues in the Pentateuch." The result of the count astonished me.

    number of words in the introductory formulas: 26
    number of words in the speeches: 289 (17×17)

A closer examination brought to light the fact that there seemed to be a numerical system by which the Primeval History was divided into three sections:

a) **The creation of human beings**
creation of male and female	Gen 1:26	17 words
creation of Eve	Gen 2:18	9 words
	Total:	26 words

b) **Crucial decisions before the flood**
to banish Adam and Eve	Gen 3:22	19 words
to limit human life span	Gen 6:3	13 words
to wipe out the human race	Gen 6:7	20 words
	Total:	52 (2×26)

   Grand total before the flood: 78 (3×26)

c) **Crucial decisions after the flood**
to spare the earth	Gen 8:21–22	23 words
to confuse language	Gen 11:6–7	28 words

   Grand total after the flood: 51 (3×17)

There seems to be a difference between the use of the numbers 17 and 26; but it is not clear why, for instance, 26 was chosen for the number of words before the flood, while 17 was selected for those after the flood. This phenomenon is not limited to the Primeval History; I have detected this variation throughout those books of the Old Testament I have analyzed numerically up till now. The structure of the text of Isaiah 59 might serve as an example of such a conscious selection of these numbers.

The first 14 verses of Isaiah 59 are clearly built up around the number 26:

verses 1–8 having	104	(4×26) words;
verses 9–14 having	78	(3×26) words;
verses 1–14 having	182	(7×26) words altogether.

However, the 7 verses 15–21 are organized around the number 17:

verses 15–18 having	51	(3×17) words;
verse 19 having	17	words;
verses 20–21 having	34	(2×17) words;
verses 15–21 having	102	(6×17) words altogether.

Further study might shed light upon the reasons for such a choice. Whatever these may be, the fact remains that we cannot ignore the numerical structure of the text when we study its literary form and its redactional history.

Let us proceed with our survey of the eleven divine monologues. The total number of words in the four remaining divine decisions (160) does not seem to have any special significance, except that the particularly crucial decision to lead the Israelites out of Egypt comprises 17 words. This is not surprising, since the total number of 289 words in all eleven speeches had to be attained, leaving no room for a multiple of 17 or 26 in the total amount of words in these four monologues. They are dealing with the divine decisions.

to inform Abraham	Gen 18:17–19	42 words
to lead Israel from Egypt	Exod 3:17	17 words
to alter Israel's route	Exod 13:17	7 words
to hide his face	Deut 32:20–27	94 words
	Total number of words:	160

The results of my inventory of the numerical aspects of the other divine addresses in the Pentateuch revealed an extraordinary high frequency of the numbers 17 and 26, which is so conspicuous that one can detect it without the help of a statistical analysis.[1] The preliminary results of these investigations have been published in a number of articles in which I did not have the pretension to offer a comprehensive survey of this complicated material. I merely intended to offer biblical scholars some insight in the use of these numbers as a structuring principle in this particular literary category.[2]

In addition to the figures already mentioned above, I shall now give a rough survey of the occurrence of these two numbers in the divine speeches in the Pentateuch. Far from claiming to treat the material exhaustively, my purpose is to give the reader an impression of their profuse use. These are the total numbers of words in divine speeches in Genesis 1–11.

all divine speeches in Gen 1:26 – 2:25	104 (4×26)
all divine speech formulas using "to say" in Gen 1–2	26
all divine speech formulas in Genesis 3	26
all divine speeches in Genesis 3–4	208 (8×26)
all divine speeches in the Story of the Flood	494 (19×26)
all divine speeches in Gen 9:8 – 11:9	156 (6×26)
all formulas and speeches in Genesis 4 (12 + 66)	78 (3×26)
all introductory divine speech formulas in Gen 1–11	102 (6×17);
the angel's address to Hagar in Gen 16:11–12	26
the angel's address to Hagar in Gen 21:17–18	26

It is interesting to note the fact that though the two addresses by the angel come from two parallel passages, which are phrased differently, they have exactly the same number of words.

Continuing our survey of the results of word counting in Genesis, we find the following.

in all divine speech formulas in Genesis 20–24	51 (3×17)
in all divine speeches together in Genesis 20–24	204 (12×17)
in all divine speeches together in Genesis 25–31	204 (12×17)
in the divine address to Rebecca in Gen 25:23	13
in the divine address to Isaac in Gen 26:2–5	55
Divine words spoken to Rebecca and Isaac:	68 (4×17)
in the address to Jacob in his dream (Gen 28:13–15)	52 (2×26)
in all divine speech formulas together in Gen 25–28	17
words to Jacob in Mesopotamia (Gen 31:3, 11–13)	51 (3×17)
words spoken to and quoted by Laban (Gen 31:24, 29)	17
words of God quoted by Jacob (Gen 32:10(9)-13(12))	17
divine oracle given to Jacob in Gen 35:10–12	26
divine oracle given to Jacob in Gen 46:3–4	26

The discovery of these numbers convinced me that 17 and 26 (and their multiples) are too consistently present in the text to be shrugged off as mere coincidence. Moreover, I realized that these numbers are a particularly dominant factor in the divine addresses in the book of Genesis. The next question regards the use of the numbers 17 and 26 in the rest of the Pentateuch.

Examples from the Book of Exodus

Investigation of the book of Exodus revealed the same compositional principles. Let me illustrate this with but one of numerous examples that could be cited.

story of Moses' birth (2:1–25; marked as Seder)	340 (20×17)
Moses' encounter with God (3:1 – 4:17; marked Seder)	650 (25X26)
all eight divine speeches together in 3:1–22	272 (16×17)
words commanded by God to be spoken to elders (3:16)	17
God's reference to his decision to set Israel free (3:17)	17
God's command to Moses to go to the king of Egypt (3:18)	26
God's promise to bring the Israelites into favor with the Egyptians (3:21–22)	26

Before we proceed with our survey, let us have a closer look at the 17 verses in which the story is told how God prepared Moses for his task (4:1–17). The reader will remember that we have already examined the seven divine speeches in this passage—see the end of chapter 3 above. Let us now carry out a more complete numerical structural analysis of this intriguing text, taking as criterion *"narrative," "introduction"* and *"divine speech."* The result is what follows.

Verses	Narrative	Introduction	Speech	
1–2	18	3	2	⎫
3	7	1	2	⎬ 26
4–5	7	4	18	⎬
6	8	4	4	⎭
7–10	9	1	43	
11–13	25	3	26	
14–17	11	1	58	
Total:	85 (5×17) +	17	+ 153 = 255 (15×17)	

The number 17 governs all three categories. The total number of words in the first four speeches is 26, as is the number of words in the sixth speech. The total number of words in the seven divine speeches, 153 (9×17), reminds us of the total amount of words in Psalm 111 and 112—see chapter 1 above under the heading "Well-known Numerical Compositions: The Alphabetic Poems," where I referred to the 153 fish mentioned in John 21:11.[3]

To show that the above passage does not stand alone, let me add two comparable texts, apart from the divine speeches in the book of Deuteronomy, which we shall examine later. The first example, Exod 15:25b-26, is structured as follows.

Narrative 7(25b) + Introduction 1(26a) + Speech 26(26ab) = 34 (2×17)

The other example, Lev 17:10–14, consists of 102 (6×17) words organized as follows:

```
Prohibition (verse 10)          22
Motivation (verse 11)           18
Introduction (verse 12a)         5 ----⎫
Speech quoted (verse 12b)       12    ⎬ 17
                                      ⎭
Instruction (verse 13)          21
Motivation (verse 14a)           7
Introduction (verse 14b)         3 ----⎫
Speech quoted (verse 14c-e)     14    ⎬ 17
                                      ⎭
                              ─────────────────
                               68  +  8  + 26 = 102
                              (4×17)  (34)  (6×17)
```

The total number of words God speaks are: 5+12 = 17 in verse 12, and 3+14 = 17 in verse 14b-e, which comes to 8+26 = 34 in the whole passage.

The Song of Moses in Exod 15:1–20, which is delimited by the Masoretes with so-called "paragraph" markers, has the following structure.

- the narrative (1a and 19) has 9+19 = 28 words
- the introduction (1a) and the song (1b-18) have 2+168 = 170 (10×17) words
- verses 1b-3 have 26 words: 9 in verse 1b and 17 in verses 2–3
- verses 11–13 have 26 words, verses 10–13 altogether 34 words
- verses 14–18 consist of 52 (2×26) words
- verses 20–21 have 26 words: 17 in the narrative and 9 in the quotation

The story about the Israelites putting the Lord to the test at Massah and Meribah in Exod 17:1–7 contains one divine speech consisting of 30 words (5–6a), which together with its 4-word introduction has 34 (2×17) words.

In the passage that follows—the story of the fight against Amalek (17:8–16)—we count exactly 119 (7×17) words.[4]

The crucial passage in Exod 19:3–8, dealing with the covenant, shows an exceptionally high frequency in the use of the numbers 17 and 26. Here are some examples.

- verses 3, 5 and 8 each have exactly 17 words.
- the divine speech in verses 3–6 consists of 51 (3×17) words.
- the divine speech in verse 9, with its introduction, has 26 words.

The situation is similar in Exodus 20, which has 26 verses.

- the passage containing the Ten Commandments, 1–17, has 17 verses
- the third commandment prohibiting the false use of God's name (Exod 20:7 and Deut 5:11) consists of 17 words
- moreover, these 17 words have a total of 51 letters
- the motivation of the sabbath rest in Exod 20:11 has 26 words
- in Deut 5:14 the commandment to stop work has 26 words

Though I could go on citing numerous other examples in the rest of the book of Exodus and in the books of Leviticus and Numbers as well, what we have presented so far must suffice to illustrate the extraordinarily high frequency of the numbers 17 and 26 and their multiples.[5]

Before we explore the numerical characteristics of the book of Deuteronomy, let me conclude the survey of the Exodus material with a brief examination of the very last chapter. I shall confine myself to 40:17–38, part of which (verses 17–33) we have studied above in regards the series of seven stereotyped formulas. As I promised there (see chapter 3 note 6), I shall now mention additional numerical aspects of these verses and of the concluding passage in 34–38. The latter passage is clearly delimited by the masoretes with a "paragraph" marker. The most important numerical characteristics are the following.

- the pericope in verses 17–33 consists of 17 verses and 208 (8×26) words
- verses 34–35, telling how the Cloud/Glory filled the Tent/Tabernacle, have 26 words
- verses 36–38, describing the function of Cloud and Fire, have 34 words
- the text of 36–38 has an unmistakable chiastic pattern
- "cloud" occurs 5× and "glory" 2×: together 7 times
- "tent" occurs 2× and "Tabernacle/tabernacling" 5×: together 7 times
- moreover, "go up" occurs 3× and "go onward" 4×: together 7 times

Conspicuous Numbers in the Divine Speeches in Deuteronomy

Since the book of Deuteronomy differs significantly from the other books of the Pentateuch both in form and content, one may wonder whether the numerical principles we detected in the divine speeches in Genesis–Numbers could be found in Deuteronomy as well. For the greater part, this book has the form of addresses by Moses, in which he often refers to words spoken by God, addressed to him or to the Israelites. Except for the divine speeches in 31:14 – 34:12, in which Moses is addressed directly, the divine speeches in Deuteronomy are *reported* speeches, references to God's speaking in the past. My investigations into these speeches showed that there was no fundamental difference between the two types of addresses in regards the use of the numbers 17 and 26.

What is rather typical of Deuteronomy is the conspicuous use of the number 10 as a structuring device. Another characteristic of this book is that in a number of cases it is difficult to distinguish between words spoken by God and words spoken by Moses. In five instances phrases are used in Moses' addresses in which God himself seems to speak in the first person singular, making it hard to decide whether such phrases should be regarded as "divine speech."[6]

However, since there appears to be no intention to quote God here as speaking personally, these cases should be interpreted as a rhetorical technique in which Moses shifts from speaking on behalf of God to speaking as if God speaks in the first person. This technique is often used in the prophetic books, especially in Jeremiah. Therefore, when I counted the number of words in the divine speeches quoted by Moses, I disregarded these instances, since such "divine words" do not fit into the category "divine speech."[7]

When I inventoried the divine speeches and introductory formulas in Deuteronomy and counted the words, I discovered that the 30 speeches were evenly divided over three main sections of the book: 10 in chapters 1–3, 10 in 4–26, and 10 in 27–34. They are structured as follows.[8]

Chapter	Introduction	Divine address	Total
1–3	31 words	463 words	494 (19×26)
4–26	27	415	442 (17×26)
27–34	27	465	492
1–34	85 words (5×17)	1343 words (79×17)	1428 words (84×17)

The obvious choice for multiples of 17 for the total number of words in both literary categories reminds us of what we have seen above in the case of Exod 4:1–17.

The use of 10 as a structuring device is typical of Deuteronomy. The reason for the use of this number is most probably the fact that the Ten Commandments play such a crucial role in the book. The number 10 was chosen to remind the attentive reader of the Constitution of the Covenant. Other instances of the use of 10 in Deuteronomy are:

- 20 instances of the phrase "YHWH our God": 10 in 1–3 and 10 in 4–26;
- 10 instances of the name YHWH in the Ten Commandments; two series of
- 10 first person plural verbs in the "we-passages" in 1–3;
- 10 instances in the book of "saying" introducing divine speech;
- 10 references to God's speaking "from the heart of the fire";
- 10 "larger literary units" in chapters 1–3;
- 10 "larger literary units" in chapters 12–26.[9]

The principle of having a particular number of words in a given category appears to be one of the intentions of the biblical writers, which I shall illustrate with additional examples below. Meanwhile, let me demonstrate this principle by examining the divine speech formulas in Deuteronomy *referring* to what God has commanded, for instance, "as the Lord had spoken / said / commanded." Such formulas appear to be pliable in the sense that they can differ in length.

"as he spoke"	2 words
"as he spoke to you"	3 words
"as the Lord spoke to me"	4 words
"as the Lord, your God, spoke to him"	5 words
"as the Lord, the God of your fathers, spoke to you"	6 words

This variation in the number of words can be explained by the desire of the author to achieve a particular number of words in a given phrase in order to attain the total number of words he needed. Thus the total number of words in the referring formulas using the verbs "to say" and "to speak" amount to 34 (2×17) in chapters 1–11 and to 26 in the rest of the book.

A survey of the use of the verb "to command" with God as subject shows that it occurs exactly 34 (2×17) times in the whole book. The total number of words in the "command-phrases" in chapters 1–11 amount to 85 (5×17), and in chapters 12–34, if I have delimited the phrases correctly, to 52 (2×26).[10]

The evidence gleaned from my study of the divine speeches in Deuteronomy corroborated what I discovered in the other

The Secret of the Hidden Sacred Numbers 17 and 26

four books of the Pentateuch. The divine speeches appear to be woven like a thread through the text in order to give it a theological structure. Moreover, there appears to be a clear predilection for the use of the two numbers 17 and 26 to give structure to the divine speeches themselves. However, there is much more to it. Subsequent investigations have shown that the evidence adduced above, impressive as it is by the massiveness of the data and the weight of the facts, is only the tip of the iceberg. My study of the numerical aspects of the 34 chapters of Deuteronomy convinced me that the entire book is a numerical composition. And this does not apply to Deuteronomy and the Pentateuch only but to other books of the Bible as well, as further probing has revealed.

Counting Verses in Deuteronomy

Having seen the numerical aspects of the divine speeches in the Pentateuch, we might wonder whether the speeches in Deuteronomy attributed to Moses have the same numerical features. There is indeed something very significant about these addresses on the level of verses. A survey of the eight main addresses by Moses directed to "all Israel," introduced by formulas using the verbs ’*amar*, "to say," and *dibber*, "to speak," gives the following picture of their number of verses.[11]

Number of verses

1.	1:6 – 4:40	147	} 676 (26×26)		
2.	5:1 – 26:19	529			
3.	27:9–10 + 28:1–68	70			
4.	29:1(2) – 30:20	48			
5.	31:2–6	5			170 (10×17)
6.	31:7–8	2	} 52 (2×26)		
7.	32:1–43	43			
8.	32:46–47	2			

The first two substantial addresses, which are of paramount importance in light of their content, are made up of 676 verses, the square number of 26.

The rest of Moses' addresses (3–8), dealing with Moses' imminent death and his succession by Joshua, are dominated by the tenfold of 17.

The last four addresses (5–8) are additionally governed by a double 26.

Though there seems to be nothing significant about the 112 verses in Deuteronomy 1–3, a survey of the number of "smaller literary units" in chapters 4–11 and the number of verses within the seven "larger literary units" reveals the following.

	Larger units	Smaller units		Verses	
1.	4:1–43	11	⎫	43 (17 + 26)	⎫
2.	5:1 – 6:3	11	⎬ 26	36	⎬ 101
3.	6:4–25	4	⎭	22 - - - - - - -	⎭
4.	7:1–26	7		26	
5.	8:1 – 9:6	7	⎫	26 - - - - - - -	⎫
6.	9:7 – 10:11	8	⎬ 26	34	⎬ 103
7.	10:12 – 11:32	11	⎭	43 (17 + 26)	⎭

What we have seen before in chapter 4 with regard to the central position of chapter 7 with its 7 "smaller literary units" in the menorah-pattern, is corroborated here on the level of both "smaller literary units" and verses. Chapter 7 is framed by 52 (2×26) "smaller literary units," 26 before and 26 after, forming a perfectly balanced pattern. The number of verses preceding chapter 7 total 101 while those following it amount to 103, totaling 204 (12×17), showing once again a (nearly perfect) balanced pattern. For a closer study of Deuteronomy 4–11 and more examples of this pattern, see chapter 6 under the heading "The Numerical Menorah-Structure and the Balance-Model."

An inventory of the number of verses in Deuteronomy 12–26, has revealed the fact that something very significant is going on here. The text appears to have been modeled upon the Ten Commandments and structured into ten "larger literary units" made up of ten sets of laws. On the level of verses they are clearly governed by the holy numbers 17 and 26.

The Secret of the Hidden Sacred Numbers 17 and 26

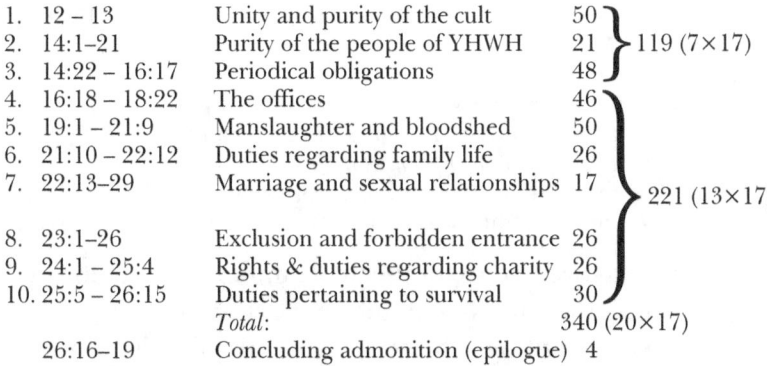

The tenth set of laws, together with the epilogue, has 34 (2×17) verses. All ten sets of laws are dominated by 17: sets 1–3 have 119 (7×17) verses and in sets 4–10 there are 221 (13×17), bringing the total to exactly 340 (20×17). Moreover, no less than four successive sets of laws, 6–9, are strikingly structured by the numbers 17 and 26.[12]

To conclude our survey of the numerical aspects of Deuteronomy on the level of verses let us examine the third major section of the book, chapters 27–34. The first part of this section, chapters 27–30, has a menorah-pattern comprising 143 verses, which do not seem to have any significant numerical features. The second part, however, chapters 31–33—in their original form without the Blessing of Moses in chapter 33, which was inserted later—is skillfully organized in a menorah-pattern with the Song of Moses at the center of a framework.[13]

A count of the verses gives the following picture.

1. 31:1–13   The outer framework A   13
2. 31:14–23   The interior framework A 10 } 17
3. 31:24–30   *The inner framework A*   7
4. 32:1–43   **The Song of Moses**   43
5. 32:44–47   *The inner framework B*   4 } 52 (2×26)
6. 32:48–52   The interior framework B   5
7. 34:1–12   **The outer framework B** 12 } 17

The survey shows the most significant numerical aspects of the Song and its framework on the level of verses, as follows.

all six sections of the entire framework together:	51 (3×17)
the Song of Moses:	43 (17+26)
2 and 3, *the interior and inner framework A:*	17
1 and 5, four speeches by Moses:	17
2 and 3, 5 and 6, the entire interior and inner framework:	26
6 and 7, *the interior and outer framework B:*	17
4, 5, 6, the Song and its inner and interior framework B:	52 (2×26)
1, 4 and 7, the outer framework A and B and the Song:	68 (4×17)

The continual occurrence of the two numbers 17 and 26 demonstrates that they are woven into the text of the Song and its framework, giving them the structural unity that is commensurate with the underlying unity of concept.

The evidence adduced above witnessing to the high frequency of occurrence of the numbers 17 and 26 and their multiples on the level of verses in Deuteronomy appears to underscore the results of our investigations on the level of words. Before proceeding to probe deeper into the way in which these two numbers were used in the biblical writings to give structure to the text, we first must address the question regarding the reason why these specific numbers appear so frequently and so numerously in the text.

The Symbolic Meaning of 17 and 26

It stands to reason that the answer to the question must be the fact that the two numbers had special significance, which can only be explained in light of their symbolic meaning. What we have discovered in the case of the use of 7, that it was its symbolic meaning as the number of fullness and abundance that made it a useful structuring tool to imbue the text with deeper significance, applies to these two numbers as well. So the real question we have to address is the question as to their symbolic meaning and function.

At the beginning of the eighties when I was doing research on the divine speeches in the Pentateuch and time and again came across these two numbers, I had no idea of their meaning. However, through the publication of my 1982 article on the pattern of the divine speech formulas, I got into communica-

The Secret of the Hidden Sacred Numbers 17 and 26

tion with the Austrian orientalist and biblical scholar Claus Schedl, whose pioneering work I shall discuss in the next chapter. Since the early sixties, he himself had independently done research on the numerical aspects of the Bible.

On the strength of the evidence that he found, he came to the conclusion that the biblical writings were numerical compositions. He was the person who inspired me most and who encouraged me to proceed with my investigations notwithstanding the negative and adverse reaction to my publications among colleagues, which he himself had also experienced with his own work. It was he who made me aware of the symbolic significance of the numbers 17 and 26, being the numbers representing the numerical value of the divine name YHWH.

As I have intimated above in chapter 1 under the heading "The Counting of Words and Verses in the Masoretic Tradition," these two numbers derive their symbolic significance from the fact that they represent, each in its own way, the presence of God through his name YHWH. The name is derived from *yahweh*, an archaized form of the *third* person singular form of *yihyeh*, "he is," of the verb *hayah*, "to be." In ancient Israel and in the Jewish tradition, the 22 letters of the Hebrew alphabet function as numerical signs, whereby each letter has a specific numerical value depending upon their position in the alphabet. The sum of the numerical values of the four letters יהוה YHWH is 26.

$$(י = 10) + (ה = 5) + (ו = 6) + (ה = 5) = 26$$

The number 17 can best be explained as the numerical value of אהוה *'ahweh*, which is analogous to the archaized form יהוה *yahweh*. The normal first person singular form of the supposed archaized form *'ahweh*, "I am," (*'ehyeh*) occurs in the famous verse in Exod 3:14, where the divine name is revealed and defined. The numerical value of אהוה *'ahweh* is 17:

$$(א = 1) + (ה = 5) + (ו = 6) + (ה = 5) = 17$$

The traditional explanation of 17 is that it is the sum of the digits of the numerical values of the letters Y H W H: 1 (+ 0) +

5 + 6 + 5 = 17. The 0-sign, which was probably unknown in biblical times, was consistently ignored in the kabbalistic tradition when it came to counting digits. In any case the two numbers have been explained as referring to the divine name in the Jewish tradition and their status of divine name numbers has been firmly established and accepted.

However, in my opinion, there is more to the symbolic significance of the two numbers in question, since they also happen to represent the numerical values of the Hebrew word *kabod*, "glory," more particularly the Glory of God, also signifying his Presence. The sum of the numerical values of the letters כבד *kbd*, since Hebrew words were written without vowel signs, adds up to 17: k = 11 + b = 2 + d = 4, but *kabod* has an additional numerical value: 26. Let me explain. The letters k to t of the Hebrew alphabet have a double function: apart from their normal alphabetical value representing the numerals 11 to 22, they were also employed to represent the tens and the hundreds: kaph = 20; lamed = 30; mem = 40; nun = 50; samekh = 60; ʿayin = 70; peh = 80; tsadeh = 90; qoph = 100; resh = 200; shin = 300; taw = 400

In accordance with these two principles the three letters of *kabod* have two numerical values.

| their alphabetical value: | k = 11 + b = 2 + d = 4 = 17 |
| their value as numerical sign: | k = 20 + b = 2 + d = 4 = 26 |

If the biblical writers were familiar with these principles, which in my opinion they were, since I do not believe that such numerical principles emerged as late as Maccabean times, they had an extra reason for using the divine name numbers. These numbers signify not only the name but also the Glory of God. So there is every reason to believe that in biblical times the two divine name numbers were closely associated with the *kabod* symbolism. The name of God and his Glory were regarded as belonging inextricably together. The intimate connection between them is most effectively demonstrated by the story in Exod 33:17–23 where Moses asks God to show him his *Glory*, but God proclaims his name.

The Secret of the Hidden Sacred Numbers 17 and 26   91

> Moses prayed: "Show me your glory." And the Lord answered: "I shall make all my goodness pass before you, and I shall pronounce in your hearing the name YHWH."

Incidentally the divine speech in verses 21–23 has 26 words: 17 in verses 21–22 and 9 in verse 23. Could these two numbers, occurring in a context in which the name and the Glory are mentioned together, have been deliberately chosen to refer symbolically to both? If so, the numerical evidence underlines the intimate relationship between God's name and his Glory. This is strikingly corroborated by the numerical features of the four passages in the Old Testament in which the words *shem*, "name," and *kabod*, "glory" (of God) are explicitly mentioned *together*, more or less as synonyms.

    Isa 59:19–21   51 (3×17) words: 17 in verse 19 and 34 in verses 20–21
    Ps 72:18–19   17 words
    Ps 102:13–23   85 (5×17) words
    Neh 9:5b   17 words spoken by the Levites

Since this cannot be mere coincidence, I interpret the consistently recurring use of the number 17, representing both the name and the Glory of God simultaneously in all five contexts, as an indication that the selection of this particular number here was intentional and premeditated by the authors.

Since *kbd* was also written with four letters: *kbwd*, the word has two additional numerical values: 23 and 32:

    alphabetical value: k = 11 + b = 2 + w = 6 + d = 4 = 23
    value as numerical sign: k = 20 + b = 2 + w = 6 + d = 4 = 32

The use of these two numbers shall be explained in chapter 6, where we shall find them in many instances.

Let us round off our answer to the question regarding the symbolic function of the numbers 17 and 26. It was once again Claus Schedl who suggested to me an explanation of the literary and theological function of these constantly occurring numbers in the text of the biblical writings. Shortly before his tragic death in an automobile accident in June 1986 he wrote to me—in what would be his very last letter—telling me that he had reread my articles about the numerical aspects of the divine speeches in the Pentateuch (cited in note 2 above). What struck him particularly was that I had brought to light the high frequency of occurrence of these two numbers, which according to him have something to do with the divine name. Referring to Gershom Scholem's book *Ursprung und Anfänge der Kabbala*, in which he briefly mentions the Jewish tradition that the name of God was interwoven in the fabric of the text of the Torah, Schedl wondered whether this "interweaving" was carried out by means of these two numbers.[14]

The Divine Name Interwoven In the Fabric of the Text

In my opinion, Schedl's suggestion offers the most plausible explanation ever put forward of the medieval kabbalistic tradition concerning the name of God interwoven in the Torah as in a fabric. The divine name numbers were the instruments employed by the biblical writers to interweave the holy name in the text of the Torah. In Schedl's opinion, we should consider the medieval tradition a reminiscence of a compositional technique that goes right back to biblical times. Therefore we must look beyond the medieval kabbalistic tradition for its origin. The relationship between the name of God and the text of the Torah did not originate in medieval kabbalistic circles. It goes back to the time of the formation of Scripture itself, the time between the Babylonian Exile and the completion of the Hebrew canon and the finalization of the text of Holy Scripture in the first century of the Common Era.[15]

Gershom Scholem refers to the kabbalistic writing *Sepher ha-Temunah*, "The book of the form," that is, the "shape," "likeness" or "representation" of the letters of the alphabet, as one of the sources for the idea of the name of God being interwoven in the Torah. The book was written most probably in Provence not later than the beginning of the thirteenth century and offers an explanation of the letters of the Hebrew alphabet on a kabbalistic basis, maintaining that the name of

God was included and preserved in a mystical way in the Torah. Scholem states that the thirteenth-century kabbalist Gikatilla was probably the first to formulate this tradition more specifically by saying that "the name of God was interwoven in the Torah as in a fabric."[16]

It is not easy to establish the precise connotation of the word Torah in this context. It might denote the Torah of Moses, the books of the Pentateuch, but it can certainly have a wider connotation signifying Holy Scripture, the entire Hebrew Bible, which I believe is the case in this context. This connotation is attested in both Jewish and Christian sources at the beginning of the Common Era. The results of my investigations into the numerical aspects of the Bible so far point definitely to a wider interpretation of the *'arigah* tradition: the name of God was interwoven in the texture not only of the Pentateuch but of the other canonical books as well. In any case we may conclude confidently that the investigations carried out thus far have established beyond any doubt the close relationship between the name of God and the biblical text. At the same time they underscore the kabbalistic tradition about the interweaving of the name in the texture of Scripture and set it in a new light.

The Purpose of the Hidden Numerical Structures

The question arises why the biblical writers made it so difficult for themselves in composing their texts. In other words, what was the purpose of the complicated numerical structures they produced in their writings. In the first place, we should realize that in antiquity the use of numbers was taken for granted in the composition of texts and was accepted as a normal compositional technique to organize a text. In biblical times, an author employed numerical devices to discipline his writing and to keep him from writing off the cuff.

In the second place, we should appreciate that numerical principles offer an author the opportunity to imbue his text with a symbolic significance and to give it an extra dimension. The structuring numbers speak a language of their own and tell their story in their own way. In virtue of the symbolism of the numbers, the texts contain a latent message hidden in the text that can only be unlocked by the reader who is familiar with such techniques or who knows how to look for these devices and find them.

In the third place, the biblical authors must have had an aesthetic aim as well: to compose works of art, literary architecture complying with their idea of perfect form and their sense of beauty. In my numerical research, I came across many passages deserving the label "compositional gem," of which I shall give a few further examples below. Psalm 19 is such a gem, in which it is said of the Torah of the Lord that it is *temimah*, "perfect" (verse 7), a term that primarily regards the contents of the Torah, but undoubtedly refers to the perfect literary form of the text as well. For the biblical authors, it was not a matter of literary beauty for the sake of beauty, but a matter of beauty in the service of the contents. Form and content belong inextricably together. In order to create such works of art, the texts were composed, irrespective of their size, according to premeditated designs suitable for the purpose and appropriate to their contents.

Claus Schedl coined the term "logotechnique" to describe the art of numerical composition, which he derived from the Greek term *logotechnia* meaning "literature," more particularly a skillfully designed literary work of art conforming to certain laws governing its form. So "logotechnique," denotes in fact "word-art," "language-art," "compositional art."[17]

Though some evident logotechnical aspects of a text may be easily detected, especially in smaller texts, they do not readily meet the eye, since they are hidden in the inmost structure of the text. The average reader cannot detect them unless he counts verses, words and other items and looks for the center of a text, knowing how to do this. However, I am not sure whether the biblical writers intended the numerical aspects of their texts to be understood and appreciated by the average reader. They knew that the artfully designed compositions could only be comprehended and prized by readers familiar with the compositional techniques, by insiders. As a matter of fact, it concerns the high technology of professional scribes, esoteric knowledge accessible to the initiated only.

It is by no means a matter of coincidence that the Hebrew word for "writing," "document" and "book," *sepher*, and the word for "scribe," *sopher*, which also means "enumerator" and "secretary," derive from one and the same verb: *sipper*, meaning both "to count," "to number" and "to recount."[18]

The "scribes" were certainly men of learning. 1 Chr 2:55 mentions families of *sopherim*, "scribes" and 2 Chr 34:13 specifies *sopherim* as Levites. They formed a professional class of craftsmen (see 1 Chr 27:32; Jer 36:26, 32 and Ps 45:1). A man of such learning and professional skill was the priest and scribe Ezra, qualified as "a scribe versed in questions concerning the commandments and the statutes of the Lord" (Ezra 7:11). The biblical scribes like Ezra were the predecessors of the *sopherim*, "the Scribes," the Pharisaic teachers of the Torah and guardians of the canonical text of the Bible, counting its verses, words and letters in order to preserve its numerical features.

We can imagine that the biblical scribes took pride in their numerical compositions. They did so in the same way as the architects and craftsmen responsible for the medieval cathedrals were proud of what they had achieved. However, such works of art were not intended primarily to satisfy the aesthetic desires and the pride of the craftsmen; they were constructed essentially to the glory of God. The scribes believed that the hidden aspects of the text, the holy numbers giving it its artful structure, which did not meet the eye of the average reader, were visible to God to whom their work was dedicated after all.

This sheds unexpected new light on one of the most enigmatic texts in the book of Deuteronomy, 29:28 in the Hebrew text (29:29 in English translations); which appears on the cover of this book, as written in the Leningrad Codex.

> The *hidden things* belong to the Lord our God; the *things revealed* belong to us and to our children for ever, that we may do all the words of this law.

The full connotation of the "hidden things" and the "things revealed" is not clear. The primary message of this verse is that in adverse and incomprehensible situations in life, that are understood only by God, the people of Israel should leave those situations to God and just keep to his commandments, which have nothing secret, enigmatic or incomprehensible about them. However, the author may also have intended to convey an additional message for those who have ears to hear. The "hidden things" *in the Torah*, the esoteric aspects of the text, are there for God's benefit to honor him; but the "things revealed," the plain and manifest features of the Torah, are there for our benefit and for that of our descendants so that we may observe them. In other words, the message is also: do not spend too much time and energy trying to discover the hidden secrets of the text, but apply yourselves to observing the prescriptions of the Torah.[19]

The Divine Name Numbers Signifying God's Presence

As I have suggested above, the purpose of the interweaving of the name of God in the texture of the biblical texts was to symbolize his presence. In biblical times, the name of God was regarded as signifying his presence in person: where God's name dwells, it was believed, he himself resides. By weaving God's name symbolically into the fabric of the text of their writings the biblical authors fitted the text with the *sign* of his presence. This does not mean, however, that they thought God was actually present in the text, so to speak contained in it. On the contrary, they fully realized that God cannot be accommodated in any object, whether it is a carved image, a book, a temple or heaven itself. The presence of God's name in the text can render it sacred but does not make it divine.

The Secret of the Hidden Sacred Numbers 17 and 26

The name is nothing but a symbol referring to God's presence among his people and witnessing to his involvement in what is said in the text.

The setting of the name in the text can best be compared with the placing of the name upon the Israelites when the priests solemnly pronounced the Aaronic blessing (Num 6:27): "They shall put my name upon the people of Israel and I will bless them."[20] God's blessing is not effectuated by some magical power emanating from his name, but by God himself, whose presence is symbolically represented by his name.[21]

In the same way, the setting of God's name in the fabric of the biblical text was not intended to imbue it with mystical features or magical powers. What the biblical writers intended was to install in the text a continuous witness to God's presence, a permanent latent message: He is here! As a matter of fact, the meaning of the name YHWH is "He is," that is, "He is present." As I have explained above, the Hebrew verbal form *yahweh*, used here as a name, is an archaized form of *yihyeh*, "he is," the normal third person singular of the verb *hayah*, "to be." The meaning of the name is defined in this way in the famous passage in Exod 3:14, where Moses asks God what he should tell the Israelites the name of his Sender was.

> And God said to Moses: "*I AM* THAT *I AM*," and He said: "This is what you shall say to the people of Israel: '*I AM* has sent me to you.'"

The text of this crucial verse in which the divine name is both revealed and explained, is meticulously structured on the level of letters so that both divine name numbers 17 and 26 are to be found in the text. Verse 14a is made up of 26 letters, divided into 15 and 11 on the basis of YH = 10 + 5 = 15 and WH = 6 + 5 = 11.

and God said to Moses, *wyʾmr ʾlhym ʾl mšh*	15 letters
"I AM THAT I AM," *ʾhyh ʾšr ʾhyh*	11 letters

Strikingly enough, verse 14b has a total of 34 (2×17) letters.

And He said: "Say this to the people of Israel: 'I AM has sent me to you'"

wyʾmr kh tʾmr lbny ysrʾl ʾhyh šlḥny ʾlykm   34 letters

This technique of using in some crucial passages even the letters to weave the divine name numbers into the text reminds us of what we have detected above: the commandment prohibiting the false use of God's name is made up of 17 words having exactly 51 (3×17) letters.

17 and 26 in the Life Spans of The Patriarchs and in the Genealogies

The presence of God, symbolized by the divine name numbers, is expressed in a particularly singular way in the names and life spans of the Hebrew patriarchs.[22] The numerical values of the names Isaac, Jacob and Joseph, which are clearly artificial literary names, are all multiples of 26.

Isaac = יצחק (י = 10) + (צ = 90) + (ח = 8) + (ק = 100) = 208 (8×26)
Jacob = יעקב (י = 10) + (ע = 70) + (ק = 100) + (ב = 2) = 182 (7×26)
Joseph = יוסף (י = 10) + (ו = 6) + (ס = 60) + (פ = 80) = 156 (6×26)

The three successive factors, 8, 7, 6, in the three multiples of 26 show a *descending* order, which expresses the hierarchical order of the three patriarchs, a technique we shall come across again presently.

Another interesting feature is that the numerical value of Sarah's alternative name *Sarai*, the only matriarch whose life span is explicitly mentioned, adds up to 510 (30×17).

Sarai = שרי   (ש = 300) + (ר = 200) + (י = 10) = 510 (30×17)

Sarah's life span of 127 years does not seem to have any symbolic meaning in itself, but perhaps this life span served another purpose. I discovered this specific function when I added her 127 years to the life spans of her husband, her son and her grandson, Abraham, Isaac and Jacob, and found that the four life spans together amount to 629 (37×17). This can

The Secret of the Hidden Sacred Numbers 17 and 26

only mean that her life span of 127 years had the function of bringing the total up to a multiple of 17.

$$
\begin{aligned}
\text{Abraham} &= 175 \\
+ \text{Isaac} &= 180 \\
+ \text{Jacob} &= \underline{147} \\
&\ 502 \\
+ \text{Sarah} &= \underline{127} \\
&\ 629
\end{aligned}
$$

Another remarkable feature is that the life spans of the three patriarchs Abraham, Isaac and Jacob, 502 years, together with Joseph's 110 years also add up to a multiple of 17, namely 612 (36×17). These data can hardly be a matter of chance, but seem to have been computed intentionally to express the relationships between these ancestors from Abraham and Sarah through to Joseph as well as the indispensability of the first Israelite matriarch.

Apart from these significant features, the life spans of the four patriarchs have another special feature: they are computed in such a way that they set the patriarchs in a striking hierarchical sequence. It was Nahum Sarna (1966) and Stanley Gevirtz (1977) who brought to the notice of the scholarly world the discovery made by Schildenberger and Meysing that the life spans of Abraham, Isaac, and Jacob appear to have been fashioned in accordance with a distinct pattern.[23] The pattern is the succession of the squares of the numbers 5, 6, and 7, having an ascending sequence ending with 7, multiplied by the uneven numbers 7, 5, and 3, starting with 7 and having a descending sequence. The three uneven numbers once again signify the hierarchy of the patriarchs.

$$
\begin{aligned}
\text{Abraham's } 175 &= 5\times5\times7 \\
\text{Isaac's } 180 &= 6\times6\times5 \\
\text{Jacob's } 147 &= 7\times7\times3
\end{aligned}
$$

James G. Williams has argued that the life span of Joseph should be included in the pattern, since Joseph symbolically brings the patriarchal narratives to an end and "combines and embodies many of the features of the portrayals of the preceding patriarchs and matriarchs." Joseph, with his life span of 110 years, is the successor in the pattern 7–5–3–1 and the sum of his predecessors multiplied by his own number in the hierarchy: $(25 + 36 + 49) \times 1 = 110$.[24]

Duane Christensen has argued that the pattern is not complete, since we are missing the formula $8 \times 8 \times 1 = 64$. Who is the fourth person in the sequence, with his 64 years? Christensen has identified this person as Israel.[25] The problem is how to explain the number 64? In my opinion, the puzzle can best be solved by calculating the numerical value of the name Israel, which adds up to exactly 64 ($10 + 21 + 20 + 1 + 12$). In this case, the number does not represent the life span of Israel (which is the same as that of Jacob), but the presence of the alternative name of Jacob.

Christensen himself has suggested another possibility based on the work of the medieval Jewish scholar Rashi. According to Rashi's calculations, Jacob left home when he was 63 years of age; but he did not go immediately to Haran. As Rashi put it, "After he had received the blessings he concealed himself in Eber's school for fourteen years."[26] Jacob served fourteen years in Laban's house for his two wives, Rachel and Leah, and another six years for Laban's flocks—before the birth of Joseph (Gen 30:25). Joseph was 30 years of age when he became ruler in Egypt, and nine years passed before Jacob came to Egypt. This would make Jacob 116 years of age when he came to Egypt, if one assumes "that the fifty-three years he spent with Laban etc. began immediately after he had left his father."[27] But Jacob himself said to Pharaoh, "[I am] 130 years [old]" (Gen 47:9)—and thus fourteen years are missing. If we follow Rashi's calculations, Jacob left Laban when he was 97 years old and spent two years en route back to Canaan. At age 99, he wrestled with the angel at the Jabbok, when his name was changed to Israel. The total of the years Jacob lived with his father Isaac and his uncle Laban was $63 + 20 = 83$ years. And since he died at 147, he lived 64 years in another "home"—14

The Secret of the Hidden Sacred Numbers 17 and 26

years in "the school of Eber," two years en route to Palestine, and 48 years as Israel in the land of Canaan and Egypt. The fourth person in the list of patriarchs according to the mathematical formula would then appear to be "Israel," as distinct from Jacob, who lived 64 years on his own—outside of his father Abraham's and his uncle Laban's house.

Abraham's 175 years are computed as: $(5 \times 5) \times 7$
Isaac's 180 years are computed as: $(6 \times 6) \times 5$
Jacob's 147 years are computed as: $(7 \times 7) \times 3$
"Israel's" 64 years are computed as: $(8 \times 8) \times 1$

Joseph's 110 years are computed as: $(5 \times 5 + 6 \times 6 + 7 \times 7) \times 1$

The question arises as to the origin of this remarkable computation. I myself have argued that the numbers 175, 180, and 147 are not to be considered the starting point of the graded arrangement of their factors but their result, since I discovered that the sum of all three sets of factors amounts to 17, which goes for the fourth set regarding "Israel" as well. This means that all four sets of factors derive from 17.

the factors of Abram's 175 years: $17 = 5 + 5 + 7$
the factors of Isaac's 180 years: $17 = 6 + 6 + 5$
the factors of Jacob's 147 years: $17 = 7 + 7 + 3$
the factors of "Israel's" 64 years: $17 = 8 + 8 + 1$

Joseph as the sum of his predecessors:

$(5 + 5) + (6 + 6) + (7 + 7) + (8 + 8) = 52 \ (2 \times 26)$

The life spans of Abraham, Isaac, and Jacob are therefore clearly governed by the divine name number 17, while that of Joseph is governed by 26, which seems to underline his distinct status and special position. The life span of Joseph, as the *sum* of his predecessors, is similar to what we found for the life span of Methuselah. I explained earlier that his 969 years is 840 (7 times the maximum of 120 years) plus the *sum* of the digits of the years mentioned with respect to Mahalalel, Jared, and Lamech (see chapter 4, "The Role of 7 in the Life Spans of the Patriarchs.")

In this way, the lives of the ancestors of the Israelites appear to be governed by the divine name numbers 17 and 26, obviously to express numerically the idea that God was with them in accordance with his promise to them. There is additional evidence to substantiate this. First, right at the beginning of the Joseph Story, in Gen 37:2, it is said that Joseph was 17 years old. Second, in Gen 47:28 the author used exactly 17 words to tell that Jacob lived in Egypt for 17 years and died at the age of 147. Finally, in the passage dealing with the death of Abraham (Gen 25:7-11) we count exactly 68 (4×17) words.

The genealogies in Genesis 10 and 11 have a number of striking numerical features. I shall confine myself to mentioning only a few to illustrate the use of the two divine name numbers 17 and 26 in the genealogies as well, once again to express God's presence and involvement. The genealogy of the sons of Noah in Genesis 10 lists the following.

- 14 descendants for Japhet and 12 for Ham, together 26
- for Shem likewise 26 descendants: 5 sons for him, 4 for Aram, 1 for Arphaxad, 1 for Shelah, 2 for Eber, and 13 for Joktan
- Mizraim's 6 sons and Canaan's 11 add up to 17 descendants
- Gen 10:21-32 consists of 104 (4×26) words and 390 (15×26) letters
- The numerical values of the names of the 10 patriarchs from Noah through Terah
- Noah, Shem, Arphaxad, Shelah, Eber, Peleg, Reu, Serug, Nahor, Terah total 3383 = 58 + 340 + 605 + 338 + 272 + 113 + 276 + 509 + 264 + 608 = 199×17
- The numerical values of Adam (45), Noah (58) and Abraham (248), the three pillars of Genesis, add up to 351, which is the sum of the numbers from 1 to 26[28]
- In Genesis 5 and 11 we count 26 names in Abraham's ancestry from Adam to Iscah
- There are 26 generations from Adam - Noah (tenth) - Abraham (twentieth) - Moses (twenty-sixth)
- In the book of Genesis exactly 26 women are mentioned by name

To show that such series of 26 are not limited to the book of Genesis, I would call attention to the fact that in the prose framework of the book of Job: the introduction (1:1 – 3:1 in the Hebrew text) and the epilogue (42:7–17), the name *YHWH* and the name *Job* both occur exactly 26 times.

Oskar Goldberg, *Die fünf Bücher Mosis ein Zahlengebäude* (Berlin, 1908), whose work I shall discuss briefly in the next chapter, has discovered that the number of letters of the 104 (4×26) words in Gen 10:21–32 is a multiple of 26, namely 390 (15×26). Moreover, he noted that the numerical values of the first 13 names add up to 3588 (138×26) and that those of the 13 sons of Joktan amount to 2756 (106×26).

The Watermark of the Name of God As the Hallmark of Holy Scripture

What I have brought forward above must suffice to give the reader an impression of the many ways in which the divine name numbers are woven into the text via names and life spans to express God's presence and involvement. Let me conclude this survey by remarking that the divine name numbers appear to have played an important role also in the formation process of Holy Scripture. With regard to the book of Psalms, Duane Christensen has discovered that at an earlier stage of its development the Psalter consisted of a collection lacking what is known as Book II, psalms 42–72, which was inserted at a later stage. This earlier collection was made up of 119 (7×17) psalms, which were structured as follows around the number 17.

Book I	(1–41)	41
Book III	(73–89)	17
Book IV	(90–106)	17
Book V	(107–150)	44

Total number of psalms: 34 + 85 = 119
(2×17) + (5×17) = (7×17)

The total number of psalms in Books I and V, 85, is a multiple of 17: (5×17), while Books III and IV each consist of 17 psalms. Moreover, of the 85 original "Davidic Psalter" (Books I and V) 51 (3×17) belong to David, while 34 (2×17) are attributed to other authors.[29] This is a clear illustration of the structuring role played by the divine name number 17 in the formation process of Scripture, of which the purpose seems to have been to "seal" the authoritative writings and preserve a canonical form of the sacred tradition.[30]

In my own research, I detected a similar role for both 17 and 26 in the formation process of the book of Deuteronomy. This means that this "sealing" of a text by means of the divine name was practiced already during the earlier stages of the growth of the text, and also at the end of that process, when the text achieved its final form. What I have observed in Deuteronomy points to a relatively early date for the use of these numbers by the biblical authors as a technique to seal their writings as holy Scripture, by fitting them, so to speak, with the watermark of the name of God, the hallmark of canonicity. Further historical research, I firmly believe, will substantiate this supposition.[31]

The Bible as a High-Grade Literary Work of Art

Investigating the Numerical Structure of the Biblical Text

Having introduced the reader in the previous chapters to the high frequency in the occurrence of the numbers 7, 17, and 26, I now intend to illustrate the structural use of these numbers which gave the biblical texts their characteristic form as numerical compositions. The numerical principles employed by their authors played a crucial role in the literary architecture of the texts and added considerably to making the Bible a high-grade work of art. The artful hand of the master composers can be detected most particularly in the refined numerical structure of the text.

When I qualify the Bible as "a work of art," I am not saying anything new, since this would be endorsed by many readers of the Bible, biblical scholars, and literary experts before me, who have discovered and come to appreciate its great literary qualities. In this respect, I have in mind specific scholars who favor a synchronic approach to the text, such as L. Alonso-Schökel and W. Richter of the "aesthetic school"; M. Weiss, who advocates a "total interpretation" from the standpoint of modern literary theory; J. Muilenburg and other advocates of "rhetorical criticism"; and the exponents of the so-called "Amsterdam school" and related circles engaged in stylistic and structural analysis.[1]

One of the basic principles held by the growing number of scholars practicing these new methods of study is the compositional unity of the biblical writings—as opposed to the dissecting diachronic approach to the biblical texts by scholars who cling to the "historical-critical" method in its old-fashioned form. Scholars of the new trend in text analysis maintain that the biblical texts, in the form they were handed down, are not the result of a haphazard formation process that came to a halt by chance, but were deliberately designed compositions. I am convinced that numerical structural analysis can both underscore and verify this cardinal tenet.

In what follows below, I shall demonstrate this conclusion by probing and revealing the numerical secrets of random samples of texts. At the same time, I shall introduce the reader to the basic principles of logotechnical or numerical structural analysis. I shall perform this within the historical context of the discipline of historical-critical text analysis, and shall therefore discuss the work of the two pioneers in this respect, Oskar Goldberg and Claus Schedl.

The numerical structural analysis of the biblical writings should not be considered a separate independent new method of studying the form of the text beside or opposite to other methods. Since the biblical writings are numerical compositions, the form of which is governed by certain numbers, the study of the form of the text should include the study of its numerical aspects. Therefore, the logotechnical analysis of a text must be regarded as part and parcel of the "literary-critical method," of which the primary objective is to study the literary form of a text; that is, the way it is structurally organized. If "literary criticism" is in fact "form criticism" in this sense, "numerical criticism" should be considered supplemental and integral to it, as I have argued and maintained from the very beginning when I introduced numerical structural analysis and integrated it into my own scholarly research.[2]

In my view, "literary criticism," the classic method of text analysis, remains the primary and absolutely indispensable way of analyzing a text and should never be replaced by other methods. Unfortunately, however, in the course of time, literary criticism has failed to address fresh questions and to adapt itself to newer insights. This resulted in one-sidedness and in the discipline getting bogged down in an excessive search for sources and layers. This development gave rise to the emergence of other methods, such as "form criticism," "rhetorical criticism" and "structural analysis," often wrongly presented as independent and diametrically different disciplines. But in my view all such methods, including "numerical structural analysis," should be regarded as supplemental to literary criticism.

The Layout Markers in The Hebrew Text of Genesis

Studying the form of the text, literary criticism, is also concerned with delimiting its "larger" and "smaller" units, the major parts and the sub-sections into which it is divided—to speak in modern terms: its chapters and paragraphs. Detecting the arrangement of a text with respect to its coherent literary units is often of crucial importance in matters of interpretation.

In the layout of the text of the Old Testament handed down in the Leningrad Codex, the oldest complete text of the Hebrew Bible (1008 CE), the Masoretes have preserved a great number of "layout markers" indicating the delimitation of its literary units. Different kinds of larger and smaller open spaces in the text were used as such "paragraph markers"—represented by a *parashah petuchah*, "open *parashah*," (P) and a *parashah setumah*, "closed *parashah*," (S) in the printed editions. Unfortunately these layout markers have in general been ignored and are still completely disregarded by the great majority of modern biblical scholars. My experience with the layout markers in the Hebrew Bible has brought to light the fact that the Masoretes have not indicated such markers consistently and fully. They seem to be absent where we would expect them. However, I am convinced that they should never be ignored in those instances where they do occur. We must keep in mind the fact that the open spaces in the layout of the text have excellent credentials going back to the time of the formation of Scripture and should never be disregarded.[3]

A notorious instance of the disregarding of the masoretic layout markers is the "paragraph marker" between verse 3 and verse 4 of Genesis 2, which has been disregarded by many commentators who think that there is a break between verse 4a and verse 4b. To make matters even worse, the editors of the printed edition, *Biblia Hebraica Stuttgartensia*, have without any justification introduced an open space at this point, which is highly misleading to scholars with no access to Codex Leningrad. There is no doubt at all that the preceding literary unit, Gen 1:1 – 2:3, with its 34 (2×17) verses, dealing with the creation of heaven and earth, ends at 2:3. The next section, dealing with the universal (hi)story of heaven and earth, more particularly that of the human race, starts at 2:4, introduced by the *toledoth*-formula: "This is the (hi)story of the heavens and the earth after their creation." Therefore, Gen 2:4–25 is not "a second creation story" but in fact the first part of the Story of the Garden of Eden (2:4 – 3:24), an insight which has consequences for its interpretation. The masoretic delimitation of 1:1 – 2:3 and 2:4–25 is rightly recognized and followed, for instance, in the *Revised English Bible*.

Another instance is the "paragraph marker" in the Masoretic Text in Job 3 between verse 1 and verse 2, which means that the literary unit dealing with the reaction of Job's three friends to his bitter plight, starting at 2:11, does not end at 2:13 but at 3:1. The only correct delimitation of this pericope is 2:11 – 3:1. This is corroborated by the numerical analysis, which shows that 3:1 belongs to the preceding section. Let us have a look at the numerical structure of Job 2:11 – 3:1 on the level of words:

verse 11:	The friends come to console him	25	
verse 12:	Their reaction upon seeing him	17	
verse 13:	They wait seven days in silence	26 { 17 } 34	
3:1:	Job breaks the silence and speaks	9	
	Total:	68 (4×17)	

The 9 words of 3:1 together with the 17 of 2:13 total 26, which demonstrates numerically that 3:1 belongs to the preceding section. This is underlined by the syntactical analysis on the basis of "main clause" and "subordinate clause," which reveals that the author has arranged his text in such a way that there are exactly 52 (2×26) words in the main clauses. Finally, it is important to note that the stereotyped introductory formula in 3:2, "And Job answered and said," introducing Job's speech, as in 6:1; 9:1; 12:1; etc., clearly indicates the beginning of a new pericope.

Returning to the book of Genesis, let us compare the occurrence of the *toledoth*-formula of Gen 2:4 with the same type of formula in 11:27, which marks the actual starting point of the Abraham cycle: "This is the (hi)story of Terah." For the interpretation of the Abraham narrative, it is crucial to know that the story starts with a short presentation of the extant tradition about the composition of Abraham's family and their journey under Terah's leadership from Ur to Haran to set out for Canaan. Taking his starting point in this tradition, the author of the Abraham story presented a theological narrative from 12:1 onwards, in which he interprets the intention of Terah to go to Canaan not as a secular enterprise, but as an act of God who called Abraham to guide him to the land he promised him.

My investigations into the use of the main layout marker, *parashah petuchah*, in the book of Genesis revealed that the book is divided into five main sections and 43 (17 + 26) sub-sections that are quite different in length. This division of the text partly overlaps the structure based upon the *toledoth* formulas, which means that the arrangement of the text visible in the layout rests upon a different conception of the structure of the contents. Whatever this conception may be, the five main sections are undoubtedly based upon the narrative cycles pertaining to the principal phases in history.

1. Creation
2. Primeval times
3. The time of Abraham
4. The time of Isaac/Jacob
5. The time of Joseph

In any case, this arrangement of the text clearly shows the structural use of the divine name numbers 17 and 26.[4]

Main sections	Sub-sections	Total number of Sub-sections
1:1 – 2:3	Creation	7 ⎫ 17 ⎫
2:4 – 10:32	Primeval cycle	10 ⎭ ⎬ 26
11:1 – 25:18	**Abraham cycle**	9 ⎫ ⎭
25:19 – 36:43	Jacob cycle	7 ⎬ 17 ⎬ 26
37:1 – 50:26	Joseph cycle	10 ⎭ ⎭

There are:
- **7 subsections in 1:1 – 2:3**: 1:1–5, 6–8, 9–13, 14–19, 20–23, 24–31; 2:1–3.
- **10 in 2:4 – 10:32**: 2:4 – 3:21; 3:22 – 4:26; 5:1–20, 21–24, 25–27; 5:28 – 6:4; 6:5–8; 6:9 – 9:17; 9:18–29; 10:1–32.
- **9 in 11:1 – 25:18**: 11:1–9; 11:10 – 12:9; 12:10 – 13:18; 14:1 – 17:27; 18:1 – 21:21; 21:22–34; 22:1–19; 22:20 – 24:67; 25:1–18.
- **7 in 25:19 – 36:43**: 25:19 – 32:3; 32:4 – 34:31; 35:1–8, 9–22, 23–29; 36:1–30, 31–43.
- **10 in 37:1 – 50:26**: 37:1–36; 38:1 – 40:23; 41:1 – 44:17; 44:18 – 46:27; 46:28 – 47:31; 48:1–22; 49:1–4, 5–12, 13–26; 49:27 – 50:26.

The function of the divine name numbers seems to be that they express the presence of God in all phases of history. The Abraham cycle, with its nine subsections, which is in the center of the five main sections, appears to be the pivotal point in this arrangement of the text. These central nine subsections, together with the 17 before the flood total 26. And together with the 17 in the Isaac-Jacob and Joseph cycle, they once again total 26.

These three examples must suffice to illustrate the importance of the layout markers and the stereotyped formulas in the text of the book of Genesis. Needless to say, what is true about Genesis also applies to the other books of the Old Testament.

The Numerical Architecture of The Hebrew Bible Rediscovered

The credit for the first attempt in modern times to draw attention to the numerical aspects of the Hebrew Bible must go to the Jewish scholar Oskar Goldberg, who presented his view of the Pentateuch as a numerical composition in 1908. On the very first page he states:[5]

> The Pentateuch is from the beginning to the end a numerical system, whose basic numbers derive from the divine name YHWH. This numerical system presents itself primarily in the contents of the text and subsequently in its style up to its most refined finesses, in fact in the entire architecture of the text divided in paragraphs, verses and parts of verses. It governs the words, determines the number of letters and becomes manifest in their numerical values as well, while the combination of these factors exhibits the fixed principle of one single number. Therefore the Pentateuch should be regarded as the unfoldment of this basic number, as the name YHWH being unfolded in a writing-in-numbers.

In order to substantiate his thesis, he studied two passages in search of their numerical aspects: the genealogy of Shem in Gen 10:21–32, and the story of the fight against Amalek in Exod 17:8–16. He discovered that the eleven verses of Gen 10:21–32 consists of 104 words, a multiple of the divine name number 26 (4×26). Having counted the letters, he found 390, which is another multiple of 26 (15×26). It appeared that there were 26 descendants of Shem. He computed the numerical values of their names and found that the first 13 names total 3588 (138×26) while the names of the 13 sons of Joktan add up to 2756 (106×26).

He counted the words of the nine verses of Exod 17:8–16 and found that they total 119, which is a multiple of the other divine name number: 7×17. The number of letters appeared to be 449, which is not a multiple of 17, but the sum of the digits (4+4+9), he noted, adds up to 17.

In addition to the numerical features of the two passages in question, which he brought to light, he drew up a long list of occurrences of the number 7 in the Pentateuch (pages 31–42). This impressive list together with the data I have referred to above should have been sufficient to demonstrate the use of the numbers 7, 17, and 26 in the Pentateuch and to underscore Goldberg's thesis. The essence of his thesis, that the Pentateuch is a numerical composition governed by the number 7 and the two divine name numbers, was clear enough to arouse at the least the interest of some biblical scholars for the numerical aspects of the Pentateuch. Nonetheless, his work appears to have been completely ignored within the main stream of scholarly research at that time. In a careful review of a number of journals from the years after 1908, I could not find any trace of, or reaction to his book.[6]

We may wonder what went wrong. In my opinion, the main reason biblical scholars did not respond to Goldberg's suggestion that the Pentateuch was a designed composition, and therefore a unity from a literary point of view, was the fact that this was not a welcome message in scholarly circles at the beginning of the twentieth century. During those days, "source- analysis," the current paradigm for explaining any "abnormalities" in the texts, reigned supreme. Scholarly research had a one-sided diachronic approach to the text that concentrated on the search for secondary additions to, and sources behind the text. Most scholars were simply not interested in an alternative approach and turned a blind eye to the possibility that the text could be a compositional unity. Moreover, the deep respect for the Masoretic Text shown by Goldberg did not square with the views of

The Bible as a High-Grade Literary Work of Art 113

the champions of textual criticism of his times who strove to establish the "original text," which was obviously not the Masoretic Text. The time was not ripe for a synchronic approach to the text, let alone for (numerical) structural analysis based upon a high regard for the masoretic textual tradition.

Another reason why not one single scholar picked up the gauntlet or gave evidence of appreciating the essence of Goldberg's thesis, is the fact that he got bogged down in typical kabbalistic exercises and led his readers away from the text into the labyrinth of the kabbalah. To give an example: the numerical value of the first 13 names of the descendants of Shem is, as we have seen, $138 \times 26 = 3588$, while the names of the 13 sons of Joktan add up to $106 \times 26 = 2756$, together: $244 \times 26 = 6344$; the sum of the digits of 6344 is $6+3+4+4 = 17$; moreover, the sum of the digits of the numerical values of the first 13 names is 177, and that of the 13 names of the sons of Joktan 218; adding up the digits of the two numbers 177 and 218 one gets $1+7+7 = 15$ and $2+1+8 = 11$; the numbers 15 and 11 represent the numerical value of YH (15) and WH (11). He also reduced the larger numbers in his numerical system not only to the two divine name numbers but ultimately to "the one and only basic number" 8 ("*die eigentliche und alleinige Grundzahl,*" page 10), which is constituted by both 17 and 26 ($1+7=8$ and $2+6=8$).

It was such exercises in higher kabbalistic mathematics that made him fail to draw the attention of the scholarly world to the numerical aspects of the biblical writings. Deterred by Goldberg's numerical acrobatic feats, his fellow scholars grasped his kabbalistic approach as a pretext to disregard his entire work and, what is more, to ignore the essence of his thesis. What they did not realize, however, was that they were "throwing the baby away with the bathwater."

Another factor that contributed to the reluctance, or even aversion, of the scholarly world to respond to Goldberg's work could have been the commotion at the turn of the century caused by Ivan Panin, who claimed that the use of the number 7 in both Old and New Testament renders the Bible a "mathematical miracle," which was supposed to prove the divine origin of its text. It is understandable that serious scholars did not want to be associated with this brand of numerology. I shall briefly refer to Panin's work and that of other champions of this claim and to Goldberg's position in chapter 7.

More importantly, Goldberg failed to make an impact on biblical scholarship because he failed to demonstrate his claim that the numerical system, governed by the divine name numbers 17 and 26 "presents itself primarily in the contents of the text and subsequently in its style up to its most refined finesses, in fact in the entire architecture of the text divided in paragraphs, verses and parts of verses." In other words, he did not show how the stylistic organization of the text was structured by these numbers. His preoccupation with medieval kabbalism gave fellow scholars the feeling that they were being led away from the text instead of towards a better understanding of its structure. Goldberg was still a long way from numerical structural analysis. It would take more than fifty years before the study of the numerical aspects of the Bible was liberated from the context of kabbalism, in which it was situated by Goldberg, and before it could become a scholarly enterprise on a scientific basis.[7]

The Pioneering Work of Claus Schedl

Numerical criticism as a new perspective for traditional literary criticism emerged when the Austrian orientalist and biblical scholar Claus Schedl set himself to seriously studying the numerical aspects of the biblical text and initiated logotechnical analysis. He was the one who would open our eyes to the ways in which the texts were given their literary form through the use of symbolic numbers as structuring devices in a variety of compositional models. As I have explained above, he was the person who coined the term "logotechnique" and who advanced and defended the thesis that the biblical writings are numerical compositions.[8]

His starting point was three principles that are deeply embedded in the Jewish tradition: first, that the letters of the alphabet have numerical values (*gematria*); second, that there is a close relationship between counting and writing; and third, the principle that there is an intimate connection between the biblical texts and counting. Leaving Goldberg's kabbalistic mathematics for what it is, he took his thesis that the Pentateuch is a numerical architecture seriously and set out to prove and substantiate his theory. Regarding it as his special assignment, he embarked upon this endeavor as a lone pioneer, scorned and ridiculed by his colleagues in biblical studies and virtually without any debating partners, except for his students in Graz. He groped his way in a totally uncharted field of study and gradually found a method to chart the numerical aspects of the Bible. By searching and registering its numerical aspects, he tried to sort out and systematize the numerical structures of the texts and to interpret the meaning of the numbers and structures he encountered.

In short, he strove to detect the architectural criteria applied by the biblical writers to give structure to their texts, by counting the number of words in a passage as a whole, in the verses and the two halves into which verses are divided. He was particularly interested in the narrative sections and direct speeches in a text, in the main clauses and subordinate clauses, and in the words describing the acts of the personages figuring in a narrative. In doing so, Schedl laid a preliminary foundation for the numerical structural analysis of biblical texts, which would form, despite its shortcomings, the basis for further research.

From a text-critical point of view it is important to note that Schedl insisted on taking one single text-tradition as the object of his numerical research and that he refrained from resorting to text-critical operations to amend this particular text. For Old Testament study he used the text handed down in *Codex Leningrad* and for the New Testament *Codex Vaticanus*, which he treated with great respect.[9] In doing so, he avoided the danger of mixing text-traditions—a widely accepted practice in biblical scholarship—and the temptation of choosing variant readings in order to achieve a text conforming to a desired numerical structure, which would of course be detrimental to the credibility of his method.

Another crucial principle for Schedl was his absolute respect for the masoretic division of the text by means of the smaller and larger open spaces, the so-called "paragraph markers," as they occur in the layout of the text of *Codex Leningrad*. He was convinced that these layout markers were not introduced in the Middle Ages but were already there in the received tradition of the masoretes in Tiberias. Moreover, he believed that the masoretic signs above some letters and words in the text and the indications in the margin had a much deeper significance than scholars were apt to think. Apart from their referring function Schedl reckoned with the possibility that they could have been used to encode some numerical aspects of the text. He was very unhappy with the way in which these signs were brought over in the modern printed editions of *Codex Leningrad* and insisted on studying the codex itself, which the great majority of scholars had not even seen at the time. Unfortunately, owing to his untimely death, he could not continue this line of research further.

His respect for the Masoretic Text tradition arose from his synchronic approach to the text and his conviction that the biblical text in its final form should be the object of our scholarly research, not some supposed earlier stage of it. This made him very critical as regards the current extremely one-sided diachronic approach to the text and the endless search for sources and earlier stages of the text as practised in literary criticism at the time. Schedl did not deny the relevance of a diachronic approach as an important historical discipline, which strictly belongs to redaction criticism. Instead he insisted that such historical research does not fit in the pursuits of literary criticism, whose sole assignment is to study the form and structure of the text in its final form.[10]

The Theoretical Foundations Of Schedl's Thesis

In order to substantiate his thesis that the biblical writings are numerical compositions, Schedl studied a number of early Jewish writings, specifically with regard to their numerical aspects, and came to the conclusion that numerical compositions are squarely embedded in Jewish culture.[11] The famous writing *Sefer Yetzirah* "Book of Creation" (first century CE) in which the "32 secret paths of wisdom" consisting of the "10 Sefirot" and the "22 elemental letters" play a significant role, contained the basic principles of Jewish number-mysticism. He regarded the formula $22 + 10 = 32$ as one of the models used for composing texts.[12]

In addition to studying early Jewish writings in search of the roots of numerical compositions, Schedl paid special attention to the role played by numbers in the mathematical-philosophical-theological worldview of the Pythagoreans and of Philo of Alexandria. This is, according to him, the cultural setting and origin of the theological insight explicitly expressed in the book *The Wisdom of Solomon*, 11:21, *Omnia in mensura et numero et pondere disposuisti*, "You (God) have arranged all things according to measure, number, and weight," which played a crucial role in our culture both in literature and architecture, in art and in music from antiquity till the rise of the romantic movement in the eighteenth and nineteenth centuries.

This is the backdrop of the idea that God as the Great Creator-Craftsman has demonstrated how creative works of art should be accomplished and that he invites us to follow suit in a kind of *imitatio Dei*. This brings to mind the clear analogy between God's creation of the world and the construction of the Tabernacle and its equipment by Moses, which we have noted above in chapter 3 under the heading "Series of Seven in the Tabernacle Laws." It also reminds us of the instructions God gave Noah for the building of the ark in the Story of the Flood, and God's command to Moses in Exod 25:9 with regard to the construction of the Tabernacle: "Make it exactly according to the design I show you" (see also verse 40). The same idea lies behind the instructions for the building of the Temple of Solomon: "All this was drafted by the Lord's own hand" (1 Chr 28:19). An earthly design should be modeled upon a heavenly plan.[13]

In view of the fact that the peoples in the ancient world were culturally interconnected, Schedl held that the ideas about the architecture of the cosmos were not only known among the Greeks but also in Babylonia. As a matter of fact, knowledge about astronomy and architecture, in which number and measure played a crucial role, had reached an advanced level in the New Babylonian Empire. It was precisely in this period, during and after the Babylonian exile, that most of the biblical writings were in the final stages of their formation. After the fall of Judah and the loss of the Temple, the scribes constructed a temple of words for their God Yahweh. Holy Scripture substituted the temple as the spiritual sanctuary, a situation that continued despite the actual rebuilding of the temple in Jerusalem.

In Schedl's opinion the scribes, who gave the religious texts their literary form, took over from the Babylonian culture a number of "building plans" governed by certain numbers functioning as formation principles, which they used to give structure to their writings. They purged the symbolism of such numbers from their pagan elements, stripped them of their polytheistic contents, and adapted them by furnishing them with new meanings. In addition to such borrowed patterns, the scribes devised literary designs of their own, such as the menorah-model and numerical patterns to seal their texts with the divine name. It was during this period that specific numerical compositional techniques were designed to give shape to sacred texts. These principles remained in vogue right through to the time of the formation of the books of the New Testament.

The Bible as a High-Grade Literary Work of Art 119

One can question Schedl's emphasis upon the supposed Babylonian influence, which I personally do. However, this does not detract anything from his thesis about the emergence of numerical compositional techniques during this period, and his discovery that the biblical writings are numerical compositions. Biblical scholars should take his thesis seriously. Objections could be raised against the fact that Schedl used a great number of symbolic numbers which gives the impression that most, if not all numbers have a symbolic function. Moreover, as H. Nobel has remarked in his critical evaluation of Schedl's work, he failed to provide his logotechnical analysis with a solid methodological basis so as to make it scientifically controllable. Nobel rightly notes, however, that this deficiency is typical of the work of a lone pioneer doing research in a totally uncharted field of study. It is up to coming generations of scholars to provide such a basis, a task that has been initiated by my research and carried a great step forward by Nobel.[14]

I am fully aware that there are still many questions to be answered regarding the origin and scope of numerical compositions in biblical times, and regarding the employment of numerical principles as a compositional technique to give structure to the texts. One cannot expect the results of the investigations carried out up till now to give adequate answers to the numerous historical questions raised by the discovery of the numerical aspects of the texts. These investigations were primarily concerned with the formal aspects of the texts—with numerical patterns and structural devices. Historical questions have not yet been addressed in any systematic way.

The present state of research can be compared with an archaeological excavation in which the foundations of an ancient city and a great number of artifacts have been laid bare. Nobody expects the archaeologist to give ready answers to the questions regarding the historical background of the discovery: who built the city, who dwelt there, and at what time, by whom and when was the city destroyed, causing it to fall into oblivion? The inability of the archaeologist to come forward with the answers to such questions does not render his discoveries void of any significance, neither does it give anybody the right to shrug off the results of the excavation.

In light of this, I consider the conclusion drawn by some reviewers of my work: "Labuschagne has not proved anything yet," unjustified. The massive amount of evidence I have brought to light sufficiently demonstrates the existence of notable numerical features of the biblical writings. The fact that I ventured to give my own interpretation of the evidence does not detract anything from the stark reality of the facts. My interpretations may be challenged, disputed, falsified, and rejected, but the hard facts I have brought to light up till now simply cannot be ignored indefinitely.

Schedl's Numerical Analysis Of New Testament Texts

The most important result of Schedl's work on the New Testament is that he demonstrated beyond any doubt that the compositional techniques he detected in the Old Testament were also employed in this corpus of Jewish-Christian literature. This discovery underscores not only the unity of the two Testaments from this angle but also confirms the Jewish character of the New Testament. Since both are products of the Jewish culture, Schedl included the New Testament texts in his logotechnical analysis as a matter of course. The results of the numerical analysis of texts I myself have chosen at random, point in the same direction. In addition to the examples I cited above, I might mention some results of my analysis of the 26 verses of John 17.

It has a clear menorah-pattern with verse 14 at the center: 1–5; 6–8; 9–13; 14; 15–19; 20–24; 25–26. Moreover, verses 1–3, which deal with the glorification of the Son and the Father, consist of 58 words, with 26 in the main clauses and 32 in the subordinate clauses. The compositional formula 26 + 32 = 58 represent the numerical value of *kebod YHWH* "the glory of the Lord." The literary unit verses 1–5 is made up of exactly 91 words, which is 7×13 (the numerical value of *'echad*, "one." Verses 7–8 have 34 (2×17) words, and both verses 12–13 and 14–16 have 51 (3×17) words each, while verses 25–26 are made up of 39 words—the numerical value of both *YHWH 'echad*, "The Lord is One," and *hashem*, "the name" (note the occurrence of *to onoma*, "the name," in verse 26!).

In earlier numerical analysis of New Testament texts by J. Smit Sibinga, former professor at the University of Amsterdam, and by his pupil M. J .J. Menken, the numerical aspects of the New Testament have been studied from a one-sided point of view. These studies have focused solely upon the Greek-Roman world, while the Jewish background has been completely disregarded. Future numerical investigations into New Testament texts could profit greatly from Schedl's work by following his broader approach in further research, which should focus particularly on the Jewish world.[15]

Significant Compositional Models Discovered by Schedl

a) The "Minor Tetraktys"

One of the most interesting compositional models discovered by Schedl is what he called the *"minor tetraktys."* A text constructed according to this model consists of 55 words with one component of 23 words and the other of 32. The term *"tetraktys"* is explained by Schedl as deriving from the Pythagorean geometric figure formed by the first four numbers: 1, as a point, with 2 forms a line, with 3 a triangle and with 4 a three-sided pyramid. The sum of these four numbers is 10, the decade, the triangular number of 4 ($1+2+3+4 = 10$). The number 55 is the triangular number of 10, or the sum of the numbers 1 through 10. In the Babylonian and Pythagorean mathematical system, these numbers were arranged in such a way that they constitute a one-dimensional equilateral triangle, or a three-dimensional pyramid. The equilateral triangle was also used in Jewish mysticism to write the three forms of the divine name, YH, YHW, and YHWH, together in one pattern, which gave rise to later kabbalistic number speculation around the letters of the Tetragrammaton.[16]

```
      1              Y
    2   3          Y H
   4  5  6         Y H W
  7 8 9 10         Y H W H
```

The numbers constituting the pyramid were divided into two groups: the first is constituted by the sum of the 4 numbers at the four corners of the pyramid: 23 (1+5+7+10), while the other group is constituted by the remaining 6 numbers forming a hexagon: 32 (2+4+8+9+6+3). This structure was frequently used by the biblical scribes as a compositional model: 23+32 = 55, of which Schedl gives a number of examples from both Old and New Testament.

In his opinion, the compositional formula 23+32 = 55 could be raised by 3: 23+32+3 = 58, or by 8: 23+32+8 = 63, or by any other number. However, 58 could also be made up of 32 and 26, representing the "glory of the Lord," *kebod YHWH*, and 63 has a symbolic value of its own, being the number of the paraenetic preaching (see my commentary, volume IA, pp. 42–43; II, p. 13, and III, pp. 221–222). As I have stated before, Schedl can be criticized for introducing too many numbers by assuming such a great number of extensions. This certainly weakens the principle. This applies also to the "cosmic" numbers identified by him, such as 19, 116, 177, 235, 243, 248, 318, 354, and 720.[17]

My own explanation of the numerical significance of the compositional formula 55 = 23+32 is that the two components represent the numerical values of the word *kabod*, "glory," alternatively written *kbwd* in the Hebrew Bible.[18] In addition to the instances mentioned by Schedl, I might give a number of examples I have discovered, one from the book of Psalms and a few more from the book of Deuteronomy.

The Bible as a High-Grade Literary Work of Art

First, Psalm 23, the poem I described as a "compositional gem," to which I have already referred with regard to the significance of the center of a text (see chapter 1 under the heading The Significance of Such Counting Activities.[19] As I explained there, a crucial theme in this psalm is the presence of God, which is symbolized in the text by the divine name number 26. The use of the "minor tetraktys" representing his "*glory*," underscores God's presence, which shows once again that there is a close relationship between content and form.

The 55 words of Psalm 23, without the heading, are divided in two different ways into 23 and 32. The number of words in the first half of each of the six verses, before the verse-divider (*ʾatnach*), total 32, while the words after the *ʾatnach* amount to 23, constituting the compositional formula 55 = 32a + 23b. Moreover, if we look at the layout of the poem in the printed edition of *Biblia Hebraica Stuttgartensia*, which is based upon the *parallellismus membrorum*, we count 32 words in the first half and 23 in the second: 55 = 32A + 23B. This means that our compositional formula has been used twice, as shown in the following table.

	a + b = Total		A + B = Total
1b	4 + 0 = 4	1b-2a	4 + 3 = 7
2	3 + 4 = 7	2b-3a	4 + 2 = 6
3	2 + 5 = 7	3b	3 + 2 = 5
4	11 + 4 = 15	4a	5 + 3 = 8
1b-4	20 + 13 = 33	1b-4a	16 + 10 = 26
		4a.b	3 + 4 = 7
5	5 + 5 = 10	5a	3 + 2 = 5
		5b	3 + 2 = 5
6	7 + 5 = 12	6a	4 + 3 = 7
		6b	3 + 2 = 5
5–6	12 + 10 = 22	4a-6	16 + 13 = 29
1b-6	32 + 23 = 55	1b-6	32 + 23 = 55

In the book of Deuteronomy, I have detected more than twenty instances of the "minor tetraktys." The first occurs in 1:9–14, with 32 words in verses 9–11, and 23 in 12–14, with an extension in verse 15 of 21 words. Such extensions are rare in my opinion. The last two occurrences of the "minor tetraktys" figure in Deuteronomy are in 31:16–21 and in 32:5–9, 7–11 and 10–14.[20] Not all of them seem to have a clearly detectable connection with the presence of God, but their use in the context suggests such a symbolic significance.

Let us examine the instances in Deuteronomy 31 and 32 in detail. The passage in chapter 31 dealing with the appearance of the Lord "as a pillar of cloud" (representing his "glory") in the Tent of Meeting to give Joshua his commission and to instruct Moses to compose the song, has some striking numerical characteristics.

Verses 14–15 are made up of 32 words, while verses 16–17 consist of 55 words, with 23 before, and 32 after the 'atnach. The three instances of the numbers representing the numerical value of *kabod*, refer appropriately to the glory and presence of the Lord in the Tent of Meeting. The final verses, 26–28, where it is told that Moses summoned the elders and officers to hear the words of the song, have a total of 55 words. However, the components 23 and 32 have not been made visible in the text, though the compositional formula 55 = 33 (words in main clauses) + 22 (words in secondary clauses) is quite near the mark.

The two *kabod*-numbers, 23 and 32, figure again very prominently in chapter 32, where Moses recites the song in the hearing of the Israelites. This does not surprise us, since Moses composed the song in the Tent of Meeting, where he experienced the glory of God's presence, as I have argued in my commentary on 31:22–23. The no less than seven occurrences of the two *kabod* numbers in 32:1–14 seem to have the function of radiating the glory of the Lord attached to Moses and the song.

The Bible as a High-Grade Literary Work of Art

There are 23 words in the narrative in verses 1–3; likewise 23 words in verses 5–6; 32 words in 7–9; 23 words in 10–11; 32 words in 13–14; moreover, there are 23 words before the ʾatnach in verses 7–10 and 32 before the ʾatnach in 7–12. The two numbers appear in pairs in verses 5–9, 7–11 and 10–14 to form three instances of the "minor tetraktys," which seem to overlap each other.

$$\left.\begin{array}{ll}\text{verses 5–6} & \text{23 words} \\ \text{verses 7–9} & \text{32 words}\end{array}\right\} 55$$

$$\left.\begin{array}{ll}\text{verses 7–9} & \text{32 words} \\ \text{verses 10–11} & \text{23 words}\end{array}\right\} 55$$

$$\left.\begin{array}{ll}\text{verses 10–11} & \text{23 words} \\ \text{verses 13–14} & \text{32 words}\end{array}\right\} 55$$

Apart from the profuse use of the *kabod* numbers 23 and 32, the two divine name numbers, 17 and 26, have been interwoven consistently into the entire text of the Song of Moses.

Chapters 33 and 34 are no exceptions to the rule; for the Blessing of Moses in 33:2–25 is made up of 272 (16×17) words with 153 (9×17) before, and 119 (7×17) after the verse divider, and the hymn in 33:26–29 has 52 (2×26) words. In 34:5–6 we count 26 words, and also in verses 7–8; in verses 9–10 there are 34 words, while verses 11–12 have 26. Surveying this in further detail would take us too far afield; therefore the reader is referred to my commentary, where a glance in the appendix will show the great number of occurrences.

Let us examine in conclusion the compositional gem in Deut 8:7–10, a Song of Praise for the Good Land, in which the "minor tetraktys" figures as a compositional formula. For the benefit of readers not versed in Hebrew, I present the text in translation. I shall refrain from presenting everything in detail and confine myself to showing how this beautiful architecture of words is carefully structured by 7, the number of fullness and abundance:

7. Since YHWH your God is bringing you into a good **LAND**[1],
—a **LAND**[2] with *streams* (1), *springs*(2), and *underground waters*(3), gushing out in valleys and hills,
8. a **LAND**[3] with wheat(1) and barley(2), vines(3), fig trees(4), and pomegranates(5),
a **LAND**[4] with oil-rich olive trees(6) and honey(7).
9. **a LAND**[5] in which you will *eat food without scarcity*(4), in which you will *lack nothing*(5); it is
a **LAND**[6] whose *stones are iron*(6), from whose hills you shall *mine copper*(7)—
10. you must eat and be sated and bless YHWH your God for the good **LAND**[7] he has given you.

Let us survey the evidence presented above.

- good LAND in verses 7 and 10 function as an *inclusion*
- the word LAND occurs 7 times in a key-word chain
- the land brings forth 7 products (verse 8)
- the land has 7 characteristics (vv. 7, 9 in italics)
- most significantly "*eat food without scarcity*" occupies center position, stressing the importance of food[21]
- the text consists of 14 (2×7) parts of sentences (main clauses and secondary clauses)
- the opening and closing sentences containing the term good LAND are made up of 7 and 7 + 3, totaling 17 words

A closer logotechnical analysis shows that the main compositional formula of the passage is 55 = 26+29, which has obviously been chosen to weave the divine name into the fabric of the text. It occurs in two different ways: in the division of the text by means of the verse divider: 55 = 26a +29b, and in its division on the basis of the criterion "main clause" (Mc) and "subordinate clause" (Sc): 55 = 29Mc+26Sc.

In addition to this, 23 words are devoted to describing the activities of the *land*, while 32 words are used to describe what God does and what the Israelites do:

The Bible as a High-Grade Literary Work of Art

```
       Total =  a + b  =  Mc + Sc  = Land + Israel + YHWH
 7.     15  =  7 +  8 =   8 + 7   =   8    +  7
 8.     10  =  6 +  4 =  10 + 0   =  10
 9.     18  = 11 +  7 =   2 +16   =   5    + 13
10.     12  =  2 + 10 =   9 + 3   =             9   +  3
        ─────────────────────────────────────────────────
        55  = 26 + 29 =  29 +26   =  23 +    29  +  3 = 32
```

b) The "Major Tetraktys"

In the formula 54 = 18+36 Schedl detected a compositional model, which he derives from the Orphic geometrical figure of the cosmic tree. The stem of the tree, the number 1, branches off into the numbers 2 and 3, which branch off, in their turn, in an arithmetical progression into their squares, 4 and 9, and cubes, 8 and 27:

$$
\begin{array}{cc}
8 = 2 \times 2 \times 2 & 3 \times 3 \times 3 = 27 \\
4 = 2 \times 2 & 3 \times 3 = 9 \\
2 & 3 \\
& 1
\end{array}
$$

The sum of the numbers 1, 2, 3, 4, 8, 9, 27 = 54, is divided into two components: 36, the sum of the numbers at the base and the top (1+8+27), and 18, the sum of the remaining numbers (2+4+3+9). This interesting model seems to occur more frequently than Schedl supposed. In addition to the example he gives in Deut 5:23–27 (*Baupläne*, p. 40 and pp. 188–190), I detected six further instances in Deuteronomy 1–11, and 4 others in chapters 12–26.[22]

c) The Pentateuch- and Decalogue-Model

Schedl derives the pattern 4+1 = 5 from the structure of the five books of the Pentateuch in which the book of Deuteronomy occupies a special position. The five chapters of the book of Lamentations, which we studied in chapter 1 above, seem to have been made up in this pattern, with four perfect alphabetic acrostics and one non-alphabetic imperfect acrostic. The final form of the book of Psalms with its five books seems to reflect this pattern, since the four books of the original Psalter, which consisted of 119 (7×17) psalms (1–41; 73–89; 90–106; 107–150), were at a later stage augmented by the insertion of Psalms 42–72, as Christensen has shown—see the last paragraph of chapter 5 above. Moreover, the New Testament Pentateuch is modeled upon this pattern: the four Gospels and the book of Acts.

The term *Decalogue-model* is derived by Schedl from the structure of the Ten Commandments, divided into 4 plus 6; but he regards the division of the geometric decade of the "minor tetraktys" as the origin of the pattern. The division of 10 into the 4 numbers at the corners of the pyramid and the remaining 6 numbers forming a hexagon—see my commentary, volume IA, 30, where I give some examples but also express some reservations.

d) The YHWH-*aechad* Model

Schedl has registered several instances of the occurrence of the compositional formula 39 = 26+13, which he labelled the YHWH-'*echad* model. Remarkably enough, it does not occur in the cardinal passage in Deut 6:4–9 containing the profession of YHWH's oneness. However, I discovered that it does occur, for instance, in 4:5–8, a passage dealing with the unity of Israel and her Torah, as well as in 4:32–35, where the theme is the oneness of YHWH's acts in history and the uniqueness of Israel's experience at Mount Horeb. It occurs several times in the story about Moses' destruction of the golden calf in 9:7 – 10:11, for instance in 9:15–17 (see my commentary, volume IB, 183–185). It also figures in 16:10–11, 22:6–7, 26:1–2, 28:68–69, 29:19–20. The last instance I found is in 33:1–3, where the compositional formula has been used twice. Particularly interesting is the frequent occurrence of 13, the numerical value of '*echad*, "one," in Deut 12:1–31, the passage about the one place of worship and the unity of the cult based upon the oneness of YHWH. The total number of words amount to 520 (40×13), with 260 (20×13) in the main clauses and 260 in the subordinate clauses. In the plural passages I counted 195 (15×13) words, and in the singular sections 325 (25×13).

In many instances where 39 words occur in a text, they are alternatively structured according to the formula 39 = 17+22, obviously to make the divine name number 17 explicit. I detected this formula, for instance, at the beginning of the book, in 3:1–2; 3:3–4; 3:8–10 and at the end in 30:1–2 and 29–30, which the reader can check in the appendices to my commentary.

The YHWH-*ʾechad* compositional formula, 39 = 26+13, appears to give structure also to the collection of the canonical books of the Old Testament. There are of course different ways of looking at the structure of the collection, depending upon the way one groups and counts them.[23]

One can count 22, by taking as one book Judges and Ruth, 1 and 2 Samuel, 1 and 2 Kings, as well as Jeremiah and Lamentations, the Twelve Minor Prophets, Ezra and Nehemiah and 1 and 2 Chronicles, which is the view of Origen and Jerome.

- ▶ 22 books can be counted in another way, by taking the five "Festal Scrolls" as a single unit—like the Book of the Twelve (minor prophets) and counting the five books of Moses, thirteen "prophets," and four "hagiographa" with Josephus.[24]
- ▶ 24 books can be counted if Ruth and Lamentations are regarded as separate books—a view found in the Talmud, 4 Ezra, and Melito.
- ▶ 27 books can be counted by splitting Samuel, Kings and Chronicles into two books each—the view expressed in the List of Bryennios, in Epiphanius, in the Septuagint, and the Vulgate.
- ▶ 39 books can be counted by regarding as two books not only 1 and 2 Samuel, 1 and 2 Kings and 1 and 2 Chronicles, but also Ezra and Nehemiah, and by counting the twelve books of the Minor Prophets separately. This is the most differentiated view of the collection and is found in most modern translations.

The 39 books, according to their arrangement in the Hebrew Bible, which differs from that of the Septuagint, Vulgate, and modern translations, show the following structure:

```
Genesis, Exodus, Leviticus, Numbers, Deuteronomy   5 ⎫
                                                     ⎬ 11 ⎫
Joshua, Judges, 1 and 2 Samuel, 1 and 2 Kings      6 ⎭    ⎬ 26 ⎫
Isaiah, Jeremiah, Ezekiel, Twelve Minor Prophets  15 ⎫    ⎭    ⎬ 39
                                                     ⎬          ⎭
Psalms, Job, Proverbs, the Five Scrolls, Daniel,     ⎪ 13 ⎭
     Ezra, Nehemiah, 1 and 2 Chronicles              ⎭
```

The 11 "historical books" and the 15 "prophetical books" represent numerically the classic division of the name in YH=15 + HW=11 = YHWH=26. Therefore, even the collection of canonical books appears to proclaim the quintessence of Israel's faith: *YHWH ʾechad*, "The Lord is one."

e) The Numerical Menorah-Structure and the Balance-Model

In the preceding chapters, we have already seen several examples of the menorah-pattern. Their main characteristic is that they are made up of seven elements: parts of sentences, sentences, verses, smaller or larger literary units. Let us now examine instances of the numerically governed menorah-pattern. The basic principle essential to this stricter specimen is the striving for symmetry and balance. As a matter of fact, symmetry and balance are the most important features of Old Testament compositional art, more particularly of Hebrew poetry. This property is manifested primarily in the *mashal*, the proverbial saying constructed in parallelism (*parallelismus membrorum*), but also in the division of verses into two halves by the ʾ*atnach*, or verse divider.

The perfect numerical menorah is symmetrical in form with a center that functions as the focal point, as we have seen in the examples adduced above. Let me illustrate this model by means of the very first menorah-pattern discovered by Claus Schedl: Deut 5:14, the prohibition of labor on the seventh day. It is made up of 26 words structured as follows:[25]

The Bible as a High-Grade Literary Work of Art

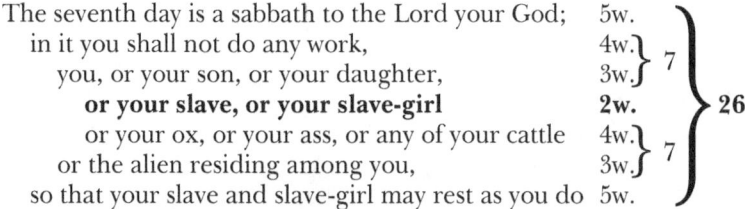

The text is structured throughout by the number 7. There are no less than six pairs having 7 words together: the first branch of the menorah, like its counterpart the seventh, together with the mathematical center have $5+2=7$ words; the second branch and its counterpart the sixth, like the second and third, and the fifth and the sixth have $4+3=7$ words; the third branch and its counterpart the fifth have $3+4=7$ words. The two words at the center are flanked by 12 words before and after. For this type of menorah, having a strict mathematical center, I have coined the term "balance-model," of which I shall give further examples from the Old Testament presently.[26]

The mentioning of the slave and slave girl at the center of the menorah is of special importance for the interpretation of the text. As the focal point this category, they receive specific emphasis, which should not surprise us, since the slave and slave girl were the most vulnerable members of the household and subject to being called upon first to carry out chores or run errands on the Sabbath. No wonder that they are explicitly referred to once again in the last sentence.

The very first numerical menorah I myself discovered is the passage in Deut 1:34–40 with its theme, the granting of permission to enter the promised land—more particularly God's refusal to grant Moses that privilege. The 7 verses are structured in a similar pattern by the numbers 34 (2×17) and 26:

Verse 34	**YHWH's reaction to the Israelites' words**	8
Verse 35	Entrance refused to the *old generation*	15 ⎫ 34
Verse 36	Entrance granted to *Caleb*	19 ⎭
Verse 37	**Entrance refused to Moses**	11
Verse 38	Entrance granted to *Joshua*	15 ⎫ 34
Verse 39	Entrance granted to the *new generation*	19 ⎭
Verse 40	**YHWH's command to the Israelites**	8

The first and last verses, which are identical in length, function as an inclusion. The second branch of the menorah and its counterpart the sixth, dealing with the old and the new generation, have together 15+19 = 34 words; so do the second and the third, about the old generation and Caleb, as well as the fifth and the sixth, dealing with Joshua and the young generation; the third branch and its counterpart the fifth, dealing with the two persons granted permission to enter, have 19+15 = 34 words; the 11 words at the center are preceded and followed by 42 (6×7) words. Moreover, the second branch and the center, dealing with the old generation and Moses, are made up of 15+11 = 26 words; so are the fifth branch and the center, dealing with Joshua and Moses: 15+11 = 26 words (the classic division of 26). In verse 37, the crucial theme of the Lord's refusal to grant Moses permission to enter the promised land occupies center position.

This theme reverberates strikingly in two further passages in Deuteronomy: in 3:23–29 and 4:20–24, both of which are structured in a similar balance-pattern.

In the 7 verses of 3:23–29, verse 26, in which Moses relates in 19 words the Lord's refusal to grant him entrance to the land, stands at the mathematical center, preceded and followed by 40 words. The 99 words are divided in 52 words before, and 47 after the *'atnach*. Moses' prayer consists of exactly 34 (2×17) words, and God's answer has 44 words, which makes a total of 78 (3×26) words in the two speeches. The Lord's command to Moses in verse 26b to refrain from raising the matter again, is made up of 9 words, while its continuation, the command to climb the mountain (verse 27) has 17 words, together 26 words.[27]

The shorter text, 4:20–24 has the same pattern: the crucial 9 words in verse 22a, "I myself am to die in this country; I shall not cross the Jordan," stand in the absolute center, preceded and followed by 35 (5×7) words.[28]

The Bible as a High-Grade Literary Work of Art

These three texts clearly demonstrate the close relationship between contents and form. Their common theme seems to require a matching structure.

Let us now examine more closely a major passage, which we have studied above on the level of verses, Deuteronomy 4–11 (see chapter 5 under "Counting Verses in Deuteronomy"). There we mentioned its near perfect balance-pattern, being made up of 204 (12×17) words divided into 7 "larger" and 59 "smaller" literary units and a block of 101 words and another of 103 words. It is structured by the 7+4 pattern and the number 26.

I	4:1–43	Warning against idolatry	7 + 4 ⎫
II	5:1 – 6:3	The crucial Horeb experience	7 + 4 ⎬ 26
III	6:4–25	The essence of Israel's faith	4 ⎭
IV	7:1–26	**Attitude towards other nations**	7
V	8:1 – 9:6	The land as God's gift	7 ⎫
VI	9:7 – 10:11	The desert drama in retrospect	8 ⎬ 26
VII	10:12 – 11:32	Preconditions for living in peace	7 + 4 ⎭

The crucial chapter 7 at the center, with its 26 verses divided over 7 "smaller units," is flanked in its larger context by 26 "smaller units." This menorah within a menorah has the following structure, based upon the contents and its numerical features.

1–4	"**Exterminate the nations!**"	66
5–6	You shall **destroy** the cult: *you are YHWH's people*!	34
7–11	*Encouragement*: God redeemed you from *Egypt*!	76
12–16	**Promise of God's blessings**.	90 ⋮ 136
17–20	*Encouragement*: remember YHWH deeds in *Egypt*!	60 (8×17)
21–24	You shall **destroy** them: *YHWH is in your midst*!	52
25–26	"**Exterminate the nations!**"	34

The first and last branches of the menorah, with their 100 words, have the same theme and function as an inclusion of the perfect symmetrically structured composition made up of 312 (12×26) words. The second branch of the menorah has 34 (2×17) words; its counterpart has 52 (2×26) words. The last branch is made up of 34 (2×17) words. The two *encouragements* in the third and fifth branches are made up of 76 + 60 = 136 (8×17) words. The promise of God's blessings is situated at the center, in pride of place.

Let me conclude the survey of the balance-pattern by mentioning some instances outside the book of Deuteronomy, to show that it is not a specific Deuteronomic compositional technique. I need not remind the reader of Psalm 23, with its mathematical center "you are with me" flanked by 26 words, which we studied in chapter 1 and referred to again above. Another significant instance in the book of Psalms is the text of Psalm 92, a "Song for the Sabbath day" (without the heading). Its 15 verses has the following structure:

```
verse 2    6  ⎫
verse 3    5  ⎬ 25  ⎫
verse 4    7  ⎭     ⎬ 52 (2×26)
verse 5    7  ⎫     ⎪
verse 6    7  ⎬ 27  ⎭
verse 7    9  ⎪
verse 8   11  ⎭
verse 9    4
verse 10  12  ⎫
verse 11   6  ⎬ 26  ⎫
verse 12   8  ⎭     ⎬ 52 (2×26)
verse 13   6  ⎫     ⎪
verse 14   6  ⎬ 26  ⎭
verse 15   6  ⎪
verse 16   8  ⎭
```

The conspicuously short verse 9, with its 4 words, is situated at the mathematical center: "you, Lord, reign for ever!" This focal point is underscored by the 7 instances of the name YHWH (in verses 2, 5, 6, 9, 10, 14, and 16) with the fourth occurrence in verse 9 at the center.

The structure of Psalm 90 is quite similar. The text of the poem itself (without the four word heading) is made up of 17 verses comprising 136 (8×17) words with 85 (5×17) before, and 51 (3×17) after the ʾatnach. The poem is divided into two equal halves: verses 1b–9 with 68 (4×17) words (42 before, and 26 after the ʾatnach), and verses 10–17 with 68 words (43 before and 25 after the ʾatnach). The mathematical center of the poem is situated between verse 9 and verse 10. However, if we include the four word heading, the mathematical center is constituted by the four words at the end of verse 9, in 9b, which convey the quintessence of the psalm: "our years die away like a murmur."

Psalm 91 is similarly divided into two numerically equal parts: verses 1–8 with 56 words, in which the poet speaks about God in the third person, and verses 9–16 with 56 words, where the author suddenly addresses God in the second person (verse 9, which reminds us of Ps 23:4). Another instance of a psalm consisting of two numerically equal halves is Psalm 79, which has 65 words in the first section (verses 1–7) and 65 in the second section. Such balance-structures do not necessarily have a clear central core.[29]

A further example is found in the seven visions of the prophet in Zechariah 1–8, with the fourth vision about the menorah and its lamps at the center, which we referred to in chapter 3, under the heading "The Significance of the Menorah in Center Position." The 14 verse passage containing the fourth vision, 4:1–14, is a menorah within a menorah. The total number of words amounts to 187 (11×17). Verse 7, with its 15 words, is situated in the mathematical center of the menorah, flanked by 86 words: 86 + 15 + 86 = 187. Incidentally 86, which is 2×43 (17+26), represents the numerical value of *'elohim*, "God," but more importantly 43 is the numerical value of the name of the central figure, Zerubbabel זרבבל: (ז=7) + (ר=20) + (ב=2) + (ב=2) + (ל=12) = 43.[30]

This brings us to our discussion of a favorite biblical compositional technique: the use of the numerical value of a name or keyword determining the number of words in the text.

Keywords Determining the Number Of Words in a Text

The reader has already been introduced to this principle of composition, when we came across the number 14 as the numerical value of the name David (14 generations) and 41 representing that of the name Abraham in Matthew 1 (41 progenitors in the genealogy, and 41 words in verses 7–9). The purpose of this technique is to underscore numerically the central idea in a text, which is in the case of Matthew 1, as we have seen, to show that Jesus is the son of Abraham and of David—see chapter 2 under "Examples from the Gospels."

This is one of numerous instances of the occurrence of this principle, which as a compositional technique is still a wholly uncharted territory. In my study of Deuteronomy, my interest in this technique was roused by the frequent occurrence of the number 38 in the passage in which it is said that "the journey from Kadesh-barnea to the crossing of the Zared lasted thirty-eight years" (2:8b-15, verse 14). The text consists of 114 words, which is 3×38. There are exactly 38 words in the "ethnographic note" in verses 10–12, and 38 words in the "we-account" (8 words in verse 8b and 9a, plus 4 words in 13b, plus 26 words in verse 14), and 38 words in the rest of the text (28 in the divine speech into which the "ethnographic note" was inserted, and 10 words in Moses' comment in verse 15).[31]

The use of the number 38 reminds us of the New Testament story about the man who had been crippled for thirty-eight years (John 5:1–18). Menken has observed that the narrative consists of 190 (5×38) words, and that up to 5:15 the discourse amounts to 76 (2×38) words, with 19 words in the rest of the discourse.[32]

Let me mention some further examples of the occurrence of this technique in Deuteronomy:

1) The numerical value of the name משה "Moses," 39 (מ=13) + (ש=21) + (ה=5) = 39, which is similar to *hashem*, "the name"!) seems to have been used in both Deut 1:1–5 and 4:44–49, two introductory "headings" which are very similar. The text of the first, preceding the introductory formula *leʾmor* at the end, consists of 78 (2×39) words, composed according to the formula 78 = 39+39+1, with 39 words before, and 39 after the verse divider (see my commentary, volume IA, 65–68). The second heading in 4:44–49 has likewise 78 words, and is structured according to the compositional formula 78 = 26a+52b, which is repeated in the syntax: 78 = 26Mc+52Sc (see volume IB, 11–13).

The Bible as a High-Grade Literary Work of Art

Moreover, we count 40 words in verses 44–46 and 38 in 47–49. This might be a coincidence, were it not that the formula 78 = 38 + 40 can be detected in 1:1–5, which means that the two crucial numbers pertaining to the journey in the desert figure prominently in both texts.

2) In 15:4–6, where God's blessing is promised, we count 54 words, the numerical value of the word *yebarekkeka*, "He will bless you" (verse 4).

3) In 16:1–4, the passage dealing with the celebration of the Passover, there are 73 words, the numerical value of *lechem ʿoni*, "bread of affliction" (verse 3).

4) In 17:16–20, where the king is ordered to make himself a copy of the Mosaic law, we find 93 words, the numerical value of *hattorah hazzot*, "this law" (verse 19), with 35 in verses 16–17 (the value of *hazzot*, "this") and 58 in 18–20 (the value of *hattorah*, "law").

5) In 19:8–10, the command not to shed innocent blood in the land, there are 60 words, the numerical value of *dam naqi*, "innocent blood" (verse 10), with exactly 17 words in the main clauses (the value of *dam*, "blood") and 43 in the subordinate clauses (the value of *naqi*, "innocent"). Moreover, the whole section 19:1–10, dealing with the sanctuary cities, consists of 186 words, the numerical value of the command in verse 7: *šaloš ʿarim tabdil lak*, "set apart three cities for you."

6) In 21:1–9, another passage dealing with the shedding of innocent blood, there are 135 words, the numerical value of *haddam hannaqi miqqereb*, "innocent blood from your midst" (verse 9).

7) In 19:14–21, in which the giving of false evidence is dealt with, we count 107 words, the numerical value of the keywords *ubiʾarta haraʿ*, "you shall rid yourself of this wickedness" (verse 19), which is made up of 66 words in the main clauses (the value of *ubiʾarta*) and 41 in the subordinate clauses (the value of *haraʿ*).

8) In 24:10–18, a passage about basic human rights (which has 119 (7×17) words), the first section, 10–13, consists of 46 words, the numerical value of the keyword *tsedaqah*, "righteousness" (verse 13).

9) Three related texts that have intrigued me in this respect are Exod 14:15–19, 23:20–23 and 33:1–3 where the "angel" or

"messenger" of the Lord is referred to. The divine speeches in both 14:15–19 and 33:1–3 have exactly 47 words, the numerical value of *mal'aki*, "my angel/messenger." This enigmatic figure is mentioned in 14:19; 33:2—where the Septuagint has "my messenger" as in 33:34 and 23:23. In 23:21, where it is said that "my name is in him," the verse is made up of 47 letters. To crown it all, the first part of the divine speech in Mal 3:19–21 (in most translations 4:1–3), introducing the promise of the coming of Elijah, consists of 47 words; the promise itself in 3:23–24 (4:5–6) has 28 words, the numerical value of Elijah (א=1 + ל=12 + י=10 + ה=5 = 28).

10) My final example comes from the book of Ecclesiastes (Qohelet), to which my attention was drawn by Duane Christensen. The book is made up of 222 verses (6X37). The number 37, which appears to govern the text, represents the numerical value of the keyword *hebel*, "vanity". Moreover, the numerical value of the five occurences of *hebel* equals 185, which is 5 X 37. This corresponds to the number of verses in what Christensen regards as the "inner frame": 92 in 2:1–6:8 plus 93 in 6:10–11:6. The 36 verses (18+18) in the "outer frame": 1:1–18 and 11:7–12:14, together with the single verse in the center of the structure (6:9) add up to 37.

Outer frame:	1:1–18		18 verses
Inner frame:	2:1 – 6:8	92 verses	
Center	**6:9**		**1 verse**
Inner frame:	6:10 – 11:6	93 verses	
Outer frame:	11:7 – 12:14		18 verses
	Total:	185 (5×37) + 37 = 222 (6×37)	

Christensen's reconstruction of the structure of the book is based upon his view of the "outer frame" and upon the supposition that 6:9 constitutes the mathematical center of the book. However, there is another way of ascertaining the structure of the text. A more plausible view of the "outer frame," in my opinion, is that it is constituted by the preamble, 1:1–11 (so delimited in the *Leningrad Codex* by means of the only *parashah petucha*, "paragraph marker," in the whole text), and the epilogue, 12:9–14. The core of the book begins with 1:12, "I, Qohelet, ruled as king over Israel in Jerusalem," and ends with 12:8, "Utter futility, says Qohelet, everything is futile." As for the center of the book: the mathematical center of the entire text is situated between 6:9 and 6:10, with 111 verses before and 111 after this point. This means that not only 6:9, but also 6:10 could be regarded as the most central verse. Thus there seems to be uncertainty about the real center of the book.

The editor responsible for the book of Ecclesiastes in the *Biblia Hebraica Stuttgartensia* took the liberty of indicating the mathematical center of the text on the level of verses between 6:9 and 6:10. He did so by using the current reference found elsewhere in the codex, *chetsi hassefer*, "center of the book," and by adding the word *bappesuqim*, meaning "in the verses." However, a glance at *Codex Leningrad* (and at Kittel's *Biblia Hebraica*) tells us that the sign in the margin signifying the center of the book and the words *chetsi hassefer*, "center of the book," are not situated at 6:9/10, but at 6:12! Moreover, there is no trace of the word *bappesuqim*, "in the verses," of which the editor gave the impression that it figures in the codex.[33]

The editor of the *Biblia Hebraica Stuttgartensia* clearly tried to "correct" the Masorah in *Codex Leningrad*, which is, to say the least, unjustified and misleading. The codex obviously represents a different view of what the "center of the book" is, or more correctly, what the Masoretes regarded as "the book" in this case: the core of the present book, 1:12 – 12:8. As Nobel has suggested, without the 17 verses of the preamble and the epilogue (the 11 verses of 1:1–11 and the 6 verses of 12:9–14), the book itself (1:12 – 12:8) is made up of 205 verses. The mathematical center of these verses constituting the core of the book, is the 103rd verse, 6:12, which appears to contain the quintessence of Qohelet's view of life:

> For who can know what is good for anyone in this life, this brief span of futile existence through which one passes like a shadow? What is to happen afterwards here under the sun, who can tell?

The *Leningrad Codex* reflects the following view of the structure of Ecclesiastes, by which the mathematical center was computed on the basis of the core of the book, 1:12 – 12:8:

The Preamble	*1:1–11*	11
First half of the book	1:12 – 6:11	102
Mathematical center	**6:12**	1
Second half of the book	7:1 – 12:8	102
The Epilogue	*12:9–14*	6
		205 + 17 = 222

The mathematically central verse of the "real" book, 6:12, is preceded by 102 (6×17) verses and followed by another 102 verses, which means that the divine name number 17 has been interwoven into the fabric of the text surrounding this central verse. Significantly, the preamble and the epilogue taken together are made up of exactly 17 verses, which appears to seal the whole book with the divine name. If there were any doubts about whether this book belongs in the canon, such doubts could have been removed by the fact that Qohelet was provided with such a watermark of canonicity.

With regard to the numerical structure of the book Qohelet, Duane Christensen has remarked: "Qohelet appears to be the most finely crafted numerical composition in the Bible."[34] Very true, though I would say "*one* of the most finely crafted numerical compositions," since there are other such compositional gems in the Bible, which render it a high-grade literary work of art, as we have seen above.

Proper Use and Misuse of Numbers in the Bible

The Significance of the Numerical Aspects of the Bible

The discovery of the numerical features of the biblical writings is first and foremost a matter that concerns the scholarly world. Its importance lies primarily in the significance it has for biblical studies. Since the numerical aspects of the text belong to its invisible inner structure, they are not apparent to the average reader of the Bible. They can only be detected by means of quantitative analysis, which is a scholarly enterprise. To this end, I have developed a standard procedure that I used in my Deuteronomy commentary to assess the quantitative aspects of the text with regard to its larger and smaller literary units, verses, and other categories relating to their form. These categories, such as "main clause" and "subordinate clause," "narrative" and "direct speech," singular and plural sections, first, second, and third person passages, are dictated by the texts themselves. In order to get an overall picture of the numerical structure of a text, one has to carry out a complete logotechnical analysis. It stands to reason that one runs the risk of over-registering because it is hard to differentiate between what was intended by the writers and what is contingent. However, such risks cannot be avoided, since we simply do not know beforehand precisely how the authors structured their texts numerically. It is only through a comprehensive quantitative analysis that the real structure of a text can be brought to light.

The discovery of such structures has far-reaching implications for our view of the form and the formation process of the biblical writings. First of all, it proves beyond any doubt that the final form of the text is not the result of a fortuitous process of haphazard accretions, but the outcome of designed compositional intention. This means that we are constrained to take the *Endgestalt* of the text more seriously than has been done by scholars working with the traditional historical-critical method. Diachronic analysis of the text should never be carried out to the detriment of a synchronic approach. Without questioning the relevance of diachronic analysis, I am convinced that the study of the final form of the text must have priority over investigations into the history of its formation. The key to understanding the distinctive or peculiar features of a text does not lie primarily in the reconstruction of the different stages of its growth, but in a careful and exhaustive examination of its final form. In my experience, many idiosyncrasies of the text can be explained as due to numerical considerations. In short, the study of the numerical aspects of a text can help us to detect its literary form.

Moreover, the numerical features of a text can help us to delimit its literary units correctly, which can have serious consequences for its interpretation. Let me demonstrate this with an example of such a crucial delimitation—Deut 8:7–10. We have examined this text in the preceding chapter and discovered that the two compositional formulas of the "minor tetraktys," $55 = 23 + 32$ and $55 = 26 + 29$, enabled us to delimit this four verse pericope precisely. Since the verses 7–10 comprise a literary unit, the next passage begins in verse 11, which means that the verb in verse 11 introduces a new literary unit: 11–16, "Take heed lest you forget the Lord your God." In other words, the protasis in 7a, "Since the Lord your God is bringing you in a good land," has its apodosis in verse 10b: "you must eat and be sated and bless YHWH your God."

The good quality of the land entails, even demands, eating, getting full, and praising the Lord. Therefore translations such as the one suggested by A. D. H. Mayes, "When the Lord brings you into the good land . . . and (when) you eat and get full and praise the Lord . . . (11) *take heed* lest you forget the Lord your God," in which the apodosis begins in verse 11, cannot be correct.[1]

How Numerical Structures Support The Message of a Text

In the previous chapters, I have presented many examples to illustrate the close connection between the form and the content of a text. I also tried to show how the numerical structure of a text can support and underscore its message. The first instance I cited, in chapter 1, was Psalm 23, in which the three words at the mathematical center of the text, *ki ʾattah ʿimmadi*, "for you are with me," are surrounded by 26 words, representing the numerical value of the divine name, to express the central idea of God's presence. Let me present some additional instances:

a) Psalm 82

In this poem, the author presents YHWH as pronouncing judgement among other gods. The psalm is made up of 61 words, consisting of 2 words in the heading and 1 word, *selah*, at the end of verse 2, and 58 words in the poem itself. The 58 words are structured as follows.

1–4 **Heavenly scene**: YHWH challenges the gods	26 ⎱ 32	
5a **The gods fail to meet YHWH's challenge**	6 ⎰	⎱ 32
5b-8 **Earthly scene**: implications for the earth	26	⎰

Exactly 26 words are used to describe the heavenly scene, in which the psalmist introduces YHWH standing in the heavenly court to pronounce judgement among the gods (verse 1). God challenges the gods in a direct address to them, in which the second person plural form is used (verses 2–4). After quoting God's address, the author describes in verse 5a the reaction of the gods to YHWH's challenge to realize justice on earth. They appear to be totally at a loss for action and unable to meet YHWH's challenge. Here the psalmist uses 6 words and employs the third person form of the verbs: "They know nothing and understand nothing, they walk about in darkness." As in Psalm 23, the sudden change in the verbal form is a clear indication of a new phase in the text.

In verse 5b, there is another significant change; for here the author speaks about the consequences that the failure of the gods has for the earth: "the foundations of the earth are all giving way." This means that from here on he has an earthly scene in mind, which he maintains throughout the rest of the poem. A further implication of the failure of the gods to meet YHWH's challenge follows as the author comes to realize that the so-called "gods" are no gods at all (verses 6–7): "I thought you were gods, all sons of the Most High, but surely like mortals you shall die and fall as any prince does." He concludes his poem by calling upon YHWH to stand up and judge the earth, in verse 8, which corresponds symmetrically to verse 1, where YHWH is presented as standing in the court of heaven to pronounce judgement among the gods.

Like the heavenly scene (verses 1–4), the earthly scene (verses 5b-8) comprises exactly 26 words. This means that the 6 words in verse 5a are at the mathematical center of the poem, where they receive special emphasis: they depict the total bankruptcy of the "gods." From a structural point of view, it does not seem to be a matter of coincidence that the description of the bankruptcy of the "gods" is situated between the heavenly and the earthly scene. The position of verse 5a in the psalm appears to be so intended as to give an appropriate indication of the position of the "gods"—who are unmasked as total failures, they are nowhere, dangling in the void between heaven and earth.[2]

The numerical structure seems to emphasize still another point: what is also at stake is YHWH's honor, which was jeopardized by the presence of the false gods. By the denouncement of these gods as non-gods on the strength of God's judgement, the honor of YHWH, the only true God, was saved. This is numerically expressed by the use of the *kebod*-YHWH model, which represents YHWH's glory and honor: 26 + 32 = 58, and its reverse, 32 + 26 = 58. Together with the 26 words dealing with the earthly scene (verses 5b-8), the 6 words of verse 5a form the compositional model 26 + 32 = 58. These same 6 words function in a pivot position, together with the 26 words of the heavenly scene (verses 1–4), where they form its reverse 32 + 26 = 58, emphasizing once again the center position of the description of the bankruptcy of the false gods.

b) Psalm 8

The similarly phrased opening and concluding lines of this hymn, "Lord, our Sovereign, how glorious is your name throughout the world," in verses 2a and 10, clearly express the purpose of the author: to sing the praise of the glorious manifestation of God's name throughout the Universe. Therefore it does not surprise us to find that the divine name numbers 17 and 26 —both of which also represent the numerical value of *kbd/kbwd*, "glory"—figure prominently in the numerical structure of the psalm. Moreover, the number 32, the alternative numerical value of *kbwd*, occurs explicitly in verse 6b.[3]

Including the 5 words of the heading, Psalm 8 is made up of 10 verses and 77 (11×7) words. The first and last lines have 7 words each. The number 7 also figures in the seven instances of the second person singular suffix -*ka*, with the reference "your name" at the beginning and at the end of the series, and with the remarkable term "your heavens" (verse 4a) at the center.

1. your name (2a)
2. your majesty (2b)
3. your adversaries (3a)
4. **your heavens (4a)**
5. your fingers (4a)
6. your hands (7a)
7. your name (10b).

The compositional formula of the hymn itself in verses 2–10, without the heading, is 72 = 38a + 34b (38 words before and 34 [2×17] after the ʾatnach). Whether it is a matter of chance or not, the number 38 represents the numerical value of *wekabod*, "and honor" (verse 6b), and 34 represents the numerical value of *shem*, "name" (ש = 21)+ (ם =13), which occurs explicitly in the first and last lines. Incidentally, 26 simultaneously represents the numerical value of *hodeka*, "your majesty" (ה = 5)+ (ו =6) + (ד =4) +(כ = 11) = 26), which appears in verse 2b.

A logotechnical analysis of the psalm brought the following structure to light.[4]

2a	**Glorification of God's name**	7
2b-3	God's achievements in the universe	15 ⎫
4–5	**Surprise at man's privileged status**	17 ⎬ 32 ⎫
6–9	God's ordination of humankind	26.... ⎭ ⎬ 58
10	**Glorification of God's name**	7

The central core of the psalm, verses 2b-9, consists of 58 words, arranged in the *kebod*-YHWH pattern: 58 = 32 + 26, with 32 words in verses 2b-5, the numerical value of *kbwd*, "glory," and with 26 words in verses 6–9, representing God's name YHWH as well as his Glory. The other divine name/Glory number (17) figures in the number of words in the exclamation of amazement about the privileged position of humankind in the universe (verses 4–5). Thus the numerical structure of the hymn underscores its central message, that the name and the Glory of God are interwoven into the fabric of the universe, where they testify to God's presence. In the same way, they are also interwoven into the fabric of Scripture, where they serve the same purpose.[5]

c) Psalm 19

It has long been recognized that this psalm divides into two distinct parts: verses 2–7, a hymn on the witness of the universe to God's work, which is strongly reminiscent of Psalm 8, and verses 8–15, a didactic poem praising the excellence of the Torah. It would be very wrong to consider the two parts as completely disparate texts, since the psalm is an incontestable structural unity. This is proved by the following logotechnical analysis, which clearly shows how the two parts have been fused to form a single entity.

Section	Contents	Number of words
2–5	The Universe proclaims God's Glory	34 (19a+15b)
6–7	The action of the sun	17
2–7	The Universe and the sun	51 (3×17)
8–11	The features of YHWH's Torah	38
6–11	The sun and the Torah	55 (32a+23b)
12–15	Concluding prayer	34 (23a+11b)
2–5 + 12–15	*Framework to the sun/Torah Hymn*	68 (42a+26b)
1–15	The psalm including its heading	126 (77a+49b)

First and foremost, the psalm is structured in terms of the number 7—the number of fullness and abundance.

- The compositional formula of the entire text contains multiples of 7: $11 \times 7 + 7 \times 7 = 18 \times 7$
- The psalm itself is made up of 14 verses.
- The name YHWH occurs 7 times (8a, 8b, 9a, 9b, 10a, 10b, 15b), with the reference to YHWH's radiant commandments (9b) at the center, hinting at the radiance of the sun.
- In verses 2–5, 7 cosmic elements are mentioned:
    1. the heavens (2a)
    2. heaven's vault (2b)
    3. day (3a)
    4. night (3b)
    5. the earth (5a)
    6. the end of the world (5a)
    7. the sun (5b)

▶ God's Torah, containing his instructions, has 14 characteristics (verses 8–11).
  1. it is perfect
  2. revives the soul
  3. is stable
  4. makes the simple wise
  5. is right
  6. rejoices the heart
  7. is radiant
  8. enlightens the eyes
  9. is pure
  10. endures for ever
  11. is true
  12. righteous
  13. more desirable than gold and fine gold
  14. sweeter than honey

At the same time the numerical structure of the text is significantly governed by the divine name number 17 in particular, but also by 26, both of which also represent God's Glory. The way they are interwoven into the text can be clearly seen in the table above. I might draw attention to a feature that has not been noted in the table, namely the dominance of the divine name numbers in the larger framework, 2–7 and 12–15, surrounding the Torah-section (8–11).

2–7	Compositional formula:	29a + 22b = 51 (3×17)
12–15	Compositional formula:	23a + 11b = 34 (2×17)
2–7 + 12–15		52a + 33b = 85 (5×17)

The occurrences of the two numbers representing the numerical values of *kabod* "glory," 23 and 32, can be detected easily. Incidentally, a significant fact is not evident in the table: verses 2–4, dealing with the proclamation of God's glory by the heavens, are made up of 23 words, while 11 words are devoted to the role of the earth (verse 5), in order to attain the number 34 (2×17).

Another significant feature of verses 6–11, the section dealing with the duo, sun and Torah, is the use of the "minor tetraktys," 55 = 32a + 23b, as a compositional formula, which demonstrates the literary unity of this section of the poem.

The primary reason why our author has chosen this particular formula, is the fact that 23 and 32 signify the glory of God. However, there is an additional reason in that 55 represents the numerical value of the word *shemesh*, "sun:" (ש = 21) + (מ = 13) + (ש = 21) = 55.

Needless to say, Psalm 19 is a high-grade numerical literary work of art. The author has made the fullest possible use of the symbolic number signifying "fullness" and the numbers representing the name and the Glory of God, in order to make his psalm a single entity. Moreover, he used these numerical techniques to underscore his message that the entire universe, in which the sun and the Torah occupy a central position, proclaims God's glorious handiwork.

d) Isa 8:19 – 9:6

My last example illustrating how the biblical authors used the numerical structure of a text to support their message is a passage in which we are faced with many problems regarding the delimitation and structure of the text and its interpretation. The passage is a difficult one in the book of Isaiah, in which the prophet proclaims a message of hope arising from the birth of a new ruler, in a desperate situation due to the Assyrian threat and the danger of a civil war during the reign of king Ahaz.

I delimit the relevant text as 8:19 – 9:6 (8:19 – 9:7 in some translations), primarily on the basis of the two masoretic layout markers, the *setumah* "paragraph marker" at the beginning and the end. The passage comprises two distinct literary units, which are juxtaposed because they are inextricably bound together by the same theme of the dawn of light in the darkness: 8:19–23 and 9:1–6 (8:19–22 and 9:1–7 in some translations).

There is much uncertainty among scholars with regard to the delimitation, more particularly, the beginning of the first subsection. The editor responsible for the book of Isaiah in *Biblia Hebraica Stuttgartensia* has added to the confusion by bringing about an open space in the text of 8:23, suggesting that a new passage begins in the middle of verse 23: "Formerly the lands of Zebulon and Naphtali were lightly regarded . . ."[6] However, in light of the layout in *Codex Leningrad*, which has no open space at this point, there is no basis for such a delimitation. In my opinion, we should follow the layout markers in the codex: the *setumah* before 8:23 and after 9:6. This delimitation is corroborated by the numerical aspects of both 8:19–23 and 9:1–6.

My logotechnical analysis of 8:19–23 has revealed the following structure.

```
8:19–23                       a +  b  = Mc + Sc = Total
19.    10 +  9 = 14 +  5 =   19    Proposition about divination
20.     2 +  9 =  6 +  5 =   11    Dawn of God's Guidance ⎫
21.     4 +  9 = 11 +  2 =   13    Distress        ⎫        ⎪
                                    and            ⎬ 23     ⎬ 32
22.     3 +  7 = 10 +  0 =   10    Darkness        ⎭        ⎪
23.    15 +  6 = 11 + 10 =   21    Honor bestowed on land ⎭

20–23  24 + 31 = 38 + 17 =   55

19–23  34 + 40 = 52 + 22 =   74
```

The literary unity of the passage is attested by the compositional formula on the basis of the verse divider, 74 = 34a + 40b (for vss 19–23) and the syntax, 55 = 24a + 31b (for vss 20–23), in which the divine name numbers 17 and 26 have been interwoven. The 74 words divide into 19 in verse 19, and 55 in verses 20–23, which signifies the presence of the "minor tetraktys" (see below).

Verse 19, should therefore be regarded as an introduction to the "minor tetraktys" in verses 20–23. It contains a proposition regarding the practice of seeking guidance through divination, which was understandably rife in those uncertain times. Taking such practices as his starting-point, the prophet presents his own guidance to the people, advising them to keep to the instructions God has given them. He points to the prospects for the future: darkness and gloom for those who rely on the diviners, but light and honor for those in anguish.

The components of the "minor tetraktys" can easily be detected, when we take the contrast between light and darkness

Proper Use and Misuse of Numbers

as the key to unlock its artfully arranged structure. In verses 21–22, which are made up of 23 words, the prophet speaks about distress, darkness, and the gloom of anguish. This part of the prophecy is surrounded by utterances about light from the Torah (verse 20), and about a situation of "no gloom" and of the "bestowing of honor" (verse 23). In the 11 words of verse 20 "dawn" is clearly the keyword: "Surely, according to this word (the citation in verse 19!) they say that there is no dawn for him (the people)." The dawn pertains to the light of guidance and salvation for those in anguish.

The 21 words of verse 23 are devoted to the bright prospects envisaged by the prophet. The total number of words in verses 20 and 23 are 32, which represents the numerical value not only of *kabod*, "glory," but also of the cognate verbal form *hikbid*, "he bestowed honor / made glorious," found in verse 23 ($hkbyd = 5+11+2+10+4 = 32$).

When I discovered this artful structure of the "minor tetraktys," I realized that the purpose of the author was to show how the light of God's guiding and saving presence encompasses the darkness, which means that the light shall overcome the darkness. It reminded me of the converse expressed in John 1:5, "The light shines in the darkness, and the darkness has not overcome it."

The number 55 also features in the compositional formula, $94 = 55a + 39b$ in 9:1–6, in which the main theme is clearly the dawn of the light of hope and salvation:

> The people that walked in darkness have seen a great light; on those who lived in a land as dark as death a light has dawned.

The passage in Isa 9:1–6 has the following structure.

```
9:1–6  a +   b  = Mc +  Sc = Total
1.      6 +  6  = 10 +   2 = 12      (third person form)......
2.      5 +  8  =  9 +   4 = 13-+⎫
3.     10 +  3  =  3 +  10 = 13-+⎬ 26 (second person)        24
4.      8 +  4  =  4 +   8 = 12      (third person form)......

1–4   29 + 21 = 26 + 24 = 50 =       26 + 24

5.     11 + 10 =  0 + 21 = 21        (third person form) ⎫
6.     15 +  8 = 18 +  5 = 23        (third person form) ⎬   44

5–6   26 + 18 = 18 + 26 = 44

1–6   55 + 39 = 44 + 50 = 94 =       26          +          68
```

The text, which divides into two parts (1–4 and 5–6), is skillfully arranged in such a way that the name/Glory-number (26) features several times in its structure, for instance, in the 26 words in the second person section (verses 2–3). The other divine name/Glory-number, 17, features in the number of words in the third person sections (verses 1, 4, 5, 6): 68 (4×17).

Particularly interesting is the syntactic compositional formula of verses 1–4, 50 = 26Mc + 24Sc (Mc = Main clause; Sc = Subordinate clause), which corresponds to the division of the 50 words into 26 in the second person section, and 24 in the third person section. The same applies to the twofold use of the compositional formula 44 = 26 + 18 in verses 5–6, where the formula 44 = 26a + 18b occurs in a reversed form in the syntactical formula 44 = 18Mc + 26Sc. Moreover, there is a third instance of this formula: the 44 words also divide into 26 in the passage in which the name of the newly born prince is specified and his reign envisaged (in italics in the translation below), and 18 in the rest of the text.

> For a child has been born to us, a son is given to us;
> he will bear the symbol of dominion on his shoulder,
> and they shall proclaim his name:
>
> *Wonderful Counselor, Mighty Hero, Eternal Father, Prince of Peace. Wide will be the dominion and boundless the peace bestowed on David's throne and on his kingdom, to establish and support it with justice and righteousness from now on, for evermore.*
>
> The zeal of the Lord of Hosts will do this.

Let me conclude the discussion by drawing attention to another significant numerical aspect of Isa 8:19 – 9:6. It concerns the use of the number 55, which not only occurs in the "minor tetraktys" giving structure to 8:20–23, but also, as we have noted, in the compositional formula of the second section of the passage (9:1–6): 94 = 55a + 39b. Apart from being the sum of 23 and 32, the number 55 appears to have a deeper significance in this particular context. In light of the likely possibility that the newborn child, referred to in 9:5, was the infant prince Hezekiah, it is not a matter of chance that the number 55 was chosen for the make-up of the text. It represents the numerical value of the name of the newborn prince חזקיהו [(ח=8) + (ז=7) + (ק=19) + (י=10) + (ה=5) + (ו=6) = 55].

In my opinion, the author's choice for the 55 words of the "minor tetraktys" was also, and perhaps primarily, motivated by his desire to embed the name of the newborn prince in the text of his prophecy. This would mean that he encoded a message in the text, expressing the messianic expectations arising from the birth of the new prince. Since it concerns a hidden message that does not meet the eye of the ordinary readers, it was known only to the prophet and to some insiders. However, it was there all the same, as a witness to his messianic expectations.

To return to where we started: the passage in question must be interpreted against the backdrop of the proposition concerning the consultation of diviners during the dark days of the reign of Ahaz. In that situation, Isaiah warned his people not to turn to mantic practices, but to listen to the word of God. As YHWH's spokesman, the prophet presents his own prophecy in opposition to that of the diviners, to offer his people guidance and hope, intimating that the newly born prince might be a messianic prince of peace.

The Misuse of Numbers by Numerologists

In view of the impending danger of misunderstanding and misusing the numerical aspects of the Bible, there is every reason to sound a warning at this point. We should exercise great caution in dealing with the function and the symbolism of numbers in the biblical writings. What we must realize at the outset, and constantly keep in mind, is the fact that biblical writers employed a limited number of symbolic numbers to give structure to their texts and, as far as I can see, an equally limited number of symbolic values to fit their texts with encoded messages. This means that we have to limit our expectations and restrict our imagination. It is wrong to assume that every number has a symbolic significance and that every text contains an encoded message. This would open the door to unrestrained speculation and arbitrary inferences.

What scholarly numerical research has brought to light is that the use of structural numbers by the biblical writers was limited to the following categories.

- ▶ the three numbers which have obtained a specific, individual symbolic significance: 7 (the number expressing fullness and abundance), to a lesser degree 10 (the useful mnemonic device expressing totality), and 11 (the number of fulfillment)
- ▶ the numbers 17 and 26, representing the numerical values of the divine name YHWH and God's *Glory*, which were interwoven into the fabric of the biblical text to express God's presence, and 23 and 32, the other two numbers representing the numerical values of *kabod* "glory," the combination of which, 23 + 32 = 55, forms the popular "minor tetraktys,"
- ▶ the numbers that derive their symbolic significance from the numerical value of a cardinal idea, or a keyword or important name occurring in some texts

As I have demonstrated above, the extremely high frequency with which the numbers 7, 11, 17, and 26 as well as the combination of 23 and 32 occur in the biblical writings shows that their occurrence is not a matter of chance or contingency, but one of design. Scribes consciously and intentionally used these numbers. The occurrence of some of the numbers that happen to have the numerical value of a cardinal idea, a keyword, or an important name in a given text could, of course,

Proper Use and Misuse of Numbers

in some cases, be a matter of chance. In the instances presented here, however, they seem to have been deliberately chosen. Their function is clearly to underscore a crucial idea in the text or to convey a message encoded in it.

However, as I have stated above, such instances are limited. Therefore, once again I must lay the greatest possible stress on the need for exercising caution in using the numerical aspects of a text to detect hidden messages and veiled predictions. Such efforts lead to the pseudo-science of numerology, a practice that goes far beyond the intentions of the biblical writers and amounts to gross misuse of the numerical aspects of the Bible. To assume the presence of an encoded message in a given text, three hard conditions have to be met.

- First, there must be a clear relation between such a message and the contents of the text—from a human point of view.
- Second, it should not fall outside the historical and cultural perspective of the biblical author.
- Third, its use by the author must be plausibly designed, reasonable, and probable. In other words, the function of the numerical aspects of a text is restricted to what the biblical writer intended.

These criteria establish the boundaries between proper use and misuse. Let me give some examples to demonstrate what I mean.[7]

In Rev 13:17–18, reference is made to the name and the number of the Beast, of which it is said "it is a human number: its number is six hundred and sixty-six." The most feasible explanation of 666 in my opinion is that it represents the numerical value of the Hebrew equivalent of Caesar Nero: QeSaR NeRoWN: Q=100 + S=60 + R=200 + N=50 + R=200 + W=6 + N=50 = 666. This interpretation fully complies with the conditions formulated above: the reference to Nero, the notorious persecutor of the early church, bears a clear relation to the contents of the book; it fits the historical and cultural context of the author and it is most plausible that he intended this veiled reference. Finally, the use of the Hebrew language in preference to Greek or Latin for computing the numerical value of Caesar Nero is compatible with the Jewish cultural background of the author.

The fact that 666 also represents the numerical value of the Roman numerals in Diocles Augustus (Diocletianus), DIoCLes aVgVstVs: D=500 + I=1 + C=100 + L=50 + V=5 + V=5 = 666, is a matter of contingency. Apart from the fact that a reference to this emperor (who lived at the end of the third century) does not square with the historical situation of the author, it is not probable that he would have used such an un-Jewish device.

The same applies to the fact that 666 also represents the numerical value of the Greek word *lateinos*, "latin": (l=30) + (a=1) + (t=300) + (e=5) + (i=10) + (n=50) + (o=70) + (s=200) = 666, which I regard as the least probable explanation.

The explanation given by the sixteenth-century Roman Catholic numerologist Peter Bungus, who interpreted the number 666 as representing the numerical value of Martin Luther (LUTHERNUC = 30 + 200 + 100 + 8 + 5 + 80 + 40 + 200 + 3 = 666), to prove that Luther was the Beast of Revelation 13, is of course bogus numerology, which has nothing whatsoever to do with the intent of the writer of Revelation.

The same goes for the assertion, which circulated during the eighties among the religious right, that Ronald Reagan was the Beast, since each of his two forenames and surname consists of 6 letters each: Ronald (6) Wilson (6) Reagan (6). What are the limits of absurdity?

Another example of the misuse of the numerical aspects of the Bible is the completely misguided, rather arrogant supposition that the Bible contains numerically coded "prophecies" pertaining to our own times. In this vein, the book of Esther is supposed to contain a coded reference to the Jewish year 5707 (707 being the numerical value of ת, ש, and ז, three Hebrew letters occurring in the names of the ten sons of Haman who were hanged: [ת=400] + [ש=300] + [ז=7] = 707). Thus it was claimed that the year 5707 (= 1946—what happened to the 5?), the year in which the Nazi war criminals were brought to justice and condemned to death by the international war crimes tribunal, was already predicted in Esther. So what?

A notorious example of numerology, based upon the Authorized Version, is mentioned by David Wells: "in Psalm 46 the forty-sixth word is "shake"; the forty-sixth word from the end counting backwards is "spear." Shakespear! Why? Well, when the King James Authorized Version was completed in 1610, Shakespear [sic!] was 46 years old!" What of it?[8]

This reminds us of the endeavours by modern computer-literate Bible freaks who subject the text of the Hebrew Bible to computer analyses in order to extract from it supposed encoded "information" regarding past, present, and future historical events, ranging from the discoveries by Edison to the rise to power of Adolf Hitler, the assassination of John F. Kennedy, the Holocaust, the presidency of Bill Clinton, the names of rabbis, the Gulf War, and the death of Yitschaq Rabin. Such exercises, which degrade the Bible to a mechanical prophesying machine, can only impress the naive and the credulous. They constitute a flagrant outrage to the biblical writers and should be rejected out of hand as totally irrelevant, and blatant nonsense.[9]

A Theological Assessment of The Numerical Aspects of the Bible

Having read what I have written in the seven chapters about the rediscovery of the astounding numerical aspects of the Bible, the reader might wonder what should be made of it. As I have stated at the beginning of this chapter, the discoveries are first and foremost a matter of concern for the scholarly world. However, since I have not written the book primarily for "specialists" but for a broader public, I shall now try to evaluate the findings on what I may call the ground level and the level of faith. During the past eighteen years, when I was invited to speak about the numerical aspects of the Bible, I was regularly confronted with the question: "What does it mean for the ordinary reader of the Bible?" My answer has always been twofold: First, that the new discoveries can arouse in us a new appreciation of the Bible as a high-grade literary work of art, our most precious heritage from antiquity. Second, that the fascinating and in some respects awe-inspiring numerical aspects of the Bible underscore the unique character of the the book that we believers assert is the Word of God.

Whether these discoveries can be interpreted as proof that the Bible is the Word of God, is quite another question. The Bible as the Word of God is a matter of faith. It does not require proof on our part. The situation is the same as regards the existence of God, which is also a matter of faith that cannot be proved in any scientific way. Therefore, in my opinion, the numerical aspects of the biblical writings, which belong to their form and style as distinct from their content, should neither be used as proof for the existence of God nor as evidence for the doctrine that the Bible is the inspired Word of God. The inspiration of the Bible concerns primarily its content, and only secondarily its form. What is said in 2 Pet 1:21, "it was under the compulsion of the Holy Spirit that people spoke as messengers of God," pertains to the message of the Bible, not to its form. The message is divine, the form is human. I might remind the reader of what I said about the interweaving of the holy divine name numbers into the fabric of the biblical texts: it renders them sacred, not divine. In other words, the content of the Bible, the substance and material dealt with in it, is divine, while its literary form and style as distinct from its content are human. Its literary form can be termed sacred but not divine in the sense of superhuman or supernatural.

This means that, despite the close relationship between the content and the form of the biblical writings, which I have amply demonstrated above, we should differentiate between the message and its form, in the same way as we differentiate the contents of a packet from its packing. The human aspects of the Bible are manifested both in its frailty and its beauty. To use a phrase from Paul's letter to the Corinthians (2 Cor 4:7): "We have this treasure in earthernware jars." They are both

Proper Use and Misuse of Numbers

frail and beautiful. The discovery of the incredibly artful numerical structures has brought to light the unsurpassed beauty of these earthernware jars. In the course of my investigations into the numerical aspects of the Bible, I was more than once deeply impressed by what I discovered. I often regarded what I found with a sense of awe, but the idea that I confronted a superhuman or supernatural phenomenon, has never crossed my mind. Though I sometimes thought "this is too beautiful not to be inspired," I have never drawn the conclusion that it cannot be the work of human beings and must therefore be ascribed to God.

Such would put God and his human agents in a most unfortunate competitive position.

Yet these discoveries have given rise to the conclusion that the Bible could not have been produced by human beings, but must have been the work of God himself. Oskar Goldberg, whose work I have discussed in chapter 6, was one of those scholars who claimed a supernatural origin for the Bible on the basis of the literary form of the Pentateuch. He regarded the awe-inspiring numerical aspects of the Torah not only as rendering it "a miracle in Antiquity" (*"ein Wunder der Urzeit"*), but also as proof of its "metaphysical origin."[10]

The most ardent and strenuous protagonist of the metaphysical origin of the Bible on the basis of its numerical aspects was Goldberg's contemporary, Ivan Panin (1855–1942), a Russian born Jew who emigrated to the New World and studied at Harvard University, where he worked as a professor of mathematics. Initially a fervent antagonist, he converted to Christianity on the basis of his study of the numerical aspects of the New Testament, more particularly his discovery of the occurrence of the number 7 and its multiples in these writings, analogous to the books of the Old Testament. His findings led him to the conclusion that the Bible as a whole is "a mathematical miracle" which could not have been produced by ordinary human beings and should therefore be regarded as God's own work. The bulk of his approximately 40,000 pages of "numerics" is devoted to kabbalistic calculations and investigations into the occurrence of the number 7, which he regarded as God's own "watermark" and which he discovered in a great number of literary and linguistic categories in both Testaments.[11]

There is no doubt that Panin actually detected a great number of such occurrences which were intentionally designed by the biblical authors, for as I have demonstrated earlier, they are indeed there. However, as a mathematician, Panin should have realized that it is relatively easy to register a great number of contingent occurrences—especially when the number of categories are unlimited—and to amass in this way an impressive number of both designed and contingent occurrences. The chance of obtaining an occurrence of 7 or a multiple in each category selected is relatively high: 1 to 7, which is more than 14 percent.

From a statistical point of view, this is one of the reasons, in my opinion, why critical scholars were not impressed by the evidence amassed by Panin. Moreover, his simplistic view of the Bible as the product of 33(!) authors, and his unscholarly, if not naive, approach to the text of the New Testament, in regarding Westcott and Hort as the most reliable, made it difficult for biblical scholars to take his work seriously. Finally, his claim regarding the metaphysical origin of the Bible on mathematical grounds, fervidly defended by himself and a horde of credulous disciples, excluded him definitively from serious, scientifically based biblical scholarship, causing all his work, including what is worthwhile in it, to be ignored. Unfortunately, but quite understandably, and inevitably, he suffered the same fate as Oskar Goldberg.

The fact that the work of both Panin and Goldberg was eclipsed does not rule out the presence of a hard core of truth in their investigations. It would be worthwhile to explore their writings to find out which discoveries could be used as scientific evidence contributing to a better understanding of biblical compositional techniques.[12]

Another prominent champion of the divine origin of the Bible in Panin's vein, was Friedrich Weinreb, a well-known but controversial figure in the Netherlands, mainly because of the dubious role he played during the war, for which he was convicted on charges of fraud and betrayal of fellow Jews. Despite this and other fraudulent practices, and due to his ability to influence, fascinate, and deceive credulous people, he had a sizeable circle of admirers particularly in the Netherlands.[13] Weinreb was a modern exponent of the Kabbalah, who used the biblical text as starting point for his cosmic number and letter speculations. His endeavors to detect the supposed hidden structure of Scripture do not contribute anything to our knowledge and understanding of the biblical writings. On the contrary, as Claus Schedl remarked, Weinreb's writings do not lead us towards the biblical text but rather away from it.

In my opinion, the rather naive idea brought forward by Goldberg, Panin, Katz, Ordman, and others—to which they are fully entitled as far as I am concerned—that the numerical features of the Bible could not possibly have been constructed by normal human computation, shows lack of respect for the mathematical capabilities and the literary craftsmanship of the biblical scribes and really amounts to slighting them. The devices the biblical scribes used were not supernatural, they were technological, falling within the competence of human beings, certainly when we consider their genius inspired. Whereas there is nothing mysterious about numbers as such, as I have stated before, there is likewise nothing mysterious in the use of numbers as a literary device to give structure to the biblical writings and to imbue them with a symbolic message.

My own reaction to the discovery of the artful numerical compositions was a considerable enhancement of my esteem for the literary craftsmanship of the biblical writers. I can confidently conclude that God bestowed exceptional gifts on these scribes, which enabled them to create such artful compositions. In the same vein, I could speak, for instance, about the medieval cathedrals and the compositions of Johann Sebastian

Bach or Wolfgang Amadeus Mozart as the inspired products of rarely gifted human beings. One does not honor God by denying what the biblical writers achieved through his gifts.

But having said all this, I would also say that there still remains an ultimate mystery about the Bible as God's inspired work that lies beyond the scope of our rational inquiry into the means he used to produce that book. The situation here is somewhat comparable to the scientific inquiry into the so-called "Big Bang" so far as the creation of the universe itself is concerned. No matter how much we learn about the process that unfolded from the moment God said, "Let there be light" (Gen 1:3), there still remains a great mystery that simply stands there—beyond the scope of scientific inquiry—invoking awe on our part.

To any reader who might conclude that my rational inquiry here on the subject of the "Bible Codes" has removed any of that ultimate mystery, I would express a word of sincere apology. I would be quick to assert that nothing is less true. Do not fear! My investigations have left the content of the biblical writings intact. What I intended was to draw your attention to the wonderful literary form of the book of books. The object of my research was the earthernware jars, not the treasure they contain, the packing, not its content. What I tried to probe was the exquisite intricacies of the biblical text, not the mystery in and behind it, that mystery that is the deepest and most profound we can experience.

I would hope that I have enabled you to look at the Bible with new eyes and to appreciate it for what it really is—from a rational point of view, our most precious literary heritage from antiquity, from the vantage point of faith, the Word of God.

Notes

A Personal Note
1 Referred to in chapter 4 note 10.
2 Cited in chapter 5 note 2.

Chapter 1: Counting Hebrew Letters, Words, and Verses in Jewish Tradition

1 For readers with a knowledge of the Dutch language, I refer to my article "De numerieke structuuranalyse van de bijbelse geschriften" in *Nederlands Theologisch Tijdschrift* 41 (1987), pp. 1–16, where I introduced the discipline of numerical criticism, which I do not regard as a new method of text analysis, but as part and parcel of literary criticism. See my contribution "De literairkritische methode," in A. S. van der Woude (ed.), *Inleiding tot de studie van het Oude Testament* (Kampen, 1986; 2nd edition 1993), pp. 102–127, in which I argued for the integration of logotechnical analysis in literary criticism.

3 See Gershom Scholem, *Kabbalah* (Jerusalem: Keter Publishing House, 1974), and *Origins of the Kabbalah*, (Philadelphia: Jewish Publication Society, 1987); and also Daniel C. Matt, *The Essential Kabbalah: the Heart of Jewish Mysticism*, (San Francisco: Harper, 1995); see Claus Schedl, *Baupläne des Wortes. Einführung in die biblische Logotechnik*, (Vienna: Herder, 1974). For Gematria see R. Weisskopf, *Gematria, Buchstabenberechnung, Tora und Schöpfung im rabbinischen Judentum* (dissertation), Tübingen 1978—see the reference in *Theologische Literaturzeitung* 105 (1980), 636–637. For the practice of gematria in Coptic Gnostic books and the New Testament, see F. B. Bond, *Gematria* (London, 1977 reprint).

4 See chapter 7 under "The Theological Assessment of the Numerical Aspects of the Bible."

5   Especially pp. 91–118; see also E. Bischoff, *Die Mystik und Magie der Zahlen* (Berlin 1920); L. Baron von Hellenbach, *Die Magie der Zahlen* (Leipzig, 1923); P. Friesenhahn, *Hellenistische Wortzahlmystik im Neuen Testament* (Leipzig-Berlin, 1936); F. C. Endres, *Mystik und Magie der Zahlen* (Zürich, 1951, 3rd ed.); and the critical works of the American mathematician E. T. Bell, *Numerology* (New York/London, 1933/1946), and *The Magic of Numbers* (London, 1946).

6   See O. Fischer, *Orientalische und griechische Zahlensymbolik* (Leipzig, 1918); A. Heller, *Biblische Zahlensymbolik* (Reutlingen, 1936), and M. H. Farbridge, *Studies in Biblical and Semitic Symbolism* (New York, 1970 reprint), especially the chapter "Symbolism of Numbers," pp. 87–156. See also the more general studies by C. Butler, *Number Symbolism* (London, 1970); M. Riemscheider, *Von 0 bis 1001. Das Geheimnis der numinosen Zahl* (Munich, 1966), and K. Menninger, *Zahlwort und Ziffer. Eine Kulturgeschichte der Zahl* (Göttingen, 1979; 3rd edition); for the Middle Ages see V. F. Hopper, *Medieval Number Symbolism. Its sources, meaning and influence on thought and expression* (New York, 1969) and particularly H. Meyer, *Die Zahlenallegorese im Mittelalter* (Munich, 1975). For the most recent comprehensive studies see Franz Carl Endres & Annemarie Schimmel, *Das Mysterium der Zahl. Zahlensymbolik im Kulturvergleich*, Eugen Diederichs Verlag (Munich, 1993; 7th edition), with an extensive systematic bibliography on pp. 297–316, and Hans A. Hutmacher, *Symbolik der biblischen Zahlen und Zeiten* (Paderborn: Verlag Ferdinand Schöning, 1993).

7   See John Allen Paulos, *Innumeracy, Mathematical Illiteracy and its Consequences* (1988); I know the Dutch version of this fascinating booklet: *Ongecijferdheid. "De gevolgen van wiskundige ongeletterdheid." "Met een nawoord van Rudy Kousbroek"* (Amsterdam: Uitgeverij Bert Bakker, 1989).

8   *Silent Poetry: Essays in Numerological Analysis*, edited by Alistair Fowler (London, 1970), p. xi. The use of "numerology" and "numerological," being associated with the occult, is most unfortunate. I prefer to use "numerical," which has no such connotation.

See also the chapter "Zahlenkomposition" in the major work by E. R. Curtius, *Europäische Literatur und lateinisches Mittelalter* (Bern-Munich, 1973; 8th edition), and R. A. Laroche, *Number Systems, Number Mysticism, and Numerical Practices in Livy (Books I-X) and Related Greek and Roman Writers* (Ph. D. Dissertation Tufts University, 1972), as well as the studies edited by A. Zimmermann, *Mensura, Mass, Zahl, Zahlensymbolik im Mittelalter*, in the series *Miscellanea Mediaevalia*, Vol. 16, 1 (1983) and 2 (1984). See also the remarks in the chapter "Getallen" by Casper Honders, *Over Bachs schouder . . .*, (Groningen, 1985), pp. 90–98. For a study on the structural use of numbers in the poetry of Dante, Milton and Spencer, see G. Quarnström, *Poetry and*

Numbers. On the Structural Use of Symbolic Numbers (Lund, 1966), and for an examination of the medieval poet Hadewijch's work see J. Bosch, Vale Milies. De structuur van Hadewijch's bundel "Strophische Gedichten," in *Tijdschrift voor Nederlandse Taal- en Letterkunde* 90 (1974), pp. 161–182.

9   *The Leningrad Codex. A Facsimile Edition* (Eerdmans: Grand Rapids, MI, and Leiden: Brill, 1998). Nearly thirty years ago a limited facsimile edition of only 135 copies, of rather mediocre quality, was published: *Pentateuch, Prophets and Hagiographa. Codex Leningrad B 19^4, the Earliest Complete Bible Manuscript* (Jerusalem: Makor Publishing, 1970), of which I was fortunate enough to obtain a copy some ten years ago.

10   Incidentally in the Pentecost passage in Acts 2:5–13 exactly 17 peoples and lands are mentioned: Galileans, Parthians, Medes, Elamites, Mesopotamia, Judaea, Cappadocia, Pontus, Asia, Phrygia, Pamphylia, Egypt, Lybia, Cyrene, Rome, Cretans and Arabs.

11   The extra verselines, 1:7 and 2:19, stand out within an otherwise regular pattern, and obviously belong to a later stage in the compositional process of the text. Excluding their 10 words gives a total of **1530** (**90×17**) words. I shall explain the significance of the number **17** and its multiple **153** in chapter 5. Note the **374** words of chapter 1, being **17×22**.

12   For further information, the reader is referred to Bo Johnson, "Form and Message in Lamentations," *Zeitschrift für die alttestamentliche Wissenschaft* 97 (1985), pp. 58–73.

13   For a study of chapter 5 see Siegfried Bergler, "Threni V—nur ein alphabetisierendes Lied? Versuch einer Deutung," *Vetus Testamentum* 27 (1977), pp. 304–320.

14   See W. Soll's entry "Acrostic" in *The Anchor Bible Dictionary*, I, pp. 58–59, where more literature is cited. For the interesting acrostic and telestic (using the terminal letters of each line) in Nahum 1, see Klaas Spronk, *Nahum:* Historical Commentary on the Old Testament (Kampen: Kok Pharos Publishing House, 1997), pp. 22–26, and especially his article "Acrostics in the book of Nahum," *Zeitschrift für die Alttestamentliche Wissenschaft* 110 (1998), pp. 209–222, in which more literature is cited. See now also Duane L. Christensen's commentary on Nahum for the Anchor Bible, Yale University Press,

2008.Chapter 2: Some Significant Numbers in the Bible

1   Exceptions to the rule are recently published writings by authors showing a marked awareness of the significance of numbers, such as P. W. Skehan, F. Langlamet, H. Rouillard, A. G. Wright, D. N. Freedman, G. Larsson, M. D. Coogan, J. Schattenmann, J. Irigoin, D. L. Christensen, L. A. Snijders, J. Smit Sibinga and M. J. J. Menken. For

particulars see my article cited in chapter 1 note 1, "De numerieke structuuranalyse van de bijbelse geschriften," especially pages 10–12.

2 I shall briefly return below to the life spans attributed to the patriarchs in chapter 4 under "The Role of 7 in the Life Spans of the Patriarchs."

3 For the readers with knowledge of Dutch I can recommend the interesting book by Dr. L. A. Snijders, *Het verhaal van de getallen in de bijbel* (Baarn, 1984), where one can find an explanation of the symbolic meaning of numbers in the Bible.

4 For the number 12 see e.g. M. H. Pope's article "Twelve" in *The Interpreter's Dictionary of the Bible*, vol. 4, p. 719, and L. A. Snijders, *op. cit.*, pp. 54–64.

5 Scholars have shown little interest in the hidden presence of the number 7 in the biblical text. In his book cited above Dr. Snijders mentions a few instances, and so does M. H. Pope in his article cited in note 3 above. However, in the lemma "Hepta" by H. Balz and G. Schneider in *Exegetisches Wörterbuch zum Neuen Testament*, Vol. II, pp. 118–119. there is no reference whatsoever to such cases. This also applies to K. H. Rengstorf's contribution "Hepta" in Gerhard Kittel's *Theologisches Wörterbuch zum Neuen Testament*, Vol. II, pp. 623–631 (*Theological Dictionary of the New Testament* (Grand Rapids, MI, 1978), pp. 627–635). The *Anchor Bible Dictionary* has no entry "Seven"; the lemma "Numbers and Counting" is not very helpful. For a general introduction to the symbolic meaning of this number, see F. C. Endres and Annemarie Schimmel, *Das Mysterium der Zahl. Zahlensymbolik im Kulturvergleich*, 7. Auflage, (München, 1984), pp.142–171 and see also pp. 313–314 where more studies are cited. See the next chapter for clusters and series of seven. It is worthwhile referring to the works of Oskar Goldberg, who has gathered many examples of such series. For a discussion and a positive evaluation of his thesis about the Pentateuch, despite his kabbalistic mathematical exercises, see below chapter 6, under the heading "The Numerical Architecture of the Hebrew Bible Rediscovered." I refer to Goldberg's book *Die fünf Bücher Mosis ein Zahlengebäude* (Berlin, 1908), pp. 31–42, and to his four articles in *La Revue Juive* 89–93 (1947), cited below in chapter 6 note 6. See now also G. Braulik's article on clusters of seven in Deuteronomy: "Die Funktion von Siebenergruppierungen im Endtext des Deuteronomium," in F. V. Reiterer (editor), *Ein Gott, eine Offenbarung*, N. Füglister Festschrift (Würzburg, 1991), pp. 37–50.

6 The origin of the symbolic meaning of 7 is discussed below, in conjunction with the numbers 4 and 11, in chapter 4 under the heading "How did 7 Acquire its Symbolic Meaning?"

7 This is the translation in the *Revised Standard Version*—see also the *King James Version*. The rendering offered by the *Revised English Bible*, "He will wear the belt of justice . . .," is misleading since it suggests an activity performed by the Messiah (wearing the belt of justice), which is not what the Hebrew text says.

8 Here again the *Revised English Bible* blurs the phrasing of the Hebrew text by leaving out the reference to the fatling (cattle). See the *Revised Standard Version* for a more accurate rendering.

9 The fact that 14 also represents the numerical value of the name Bach, according to the position of the four letters in the alphabet $(2+1+3+8 = 14)$, is of course pure coincidence. The reason why I refer to Johann Sebastian Bach in the present context is to remind the reader that Bach in particular was aware of the potential of numbers to imbue musical compositions with symbolism. See Ruth Tatlow, *Bach and the Riddle of the Number Alphabet* (Cambridge, 1991), as well as Casper Honders, *Over Bachs Schouder* (Groningen, 1985), pp. 90–98. The book written by Kees van Houten and Marinus Kasbergen, *Bach en het Getal*, Zutphen 1985, claims more than could possibly be verified—see Casper Honders' review in *Het Orgel* (Journal of the Dutch Society of Organists), 81/6 (1985), pp. 317–322 and that of A. M. M. Dekker in *Nederlands Archief voor Kerkgeschiedenis*, 70 (1990), pp. 115–117.

10 For a more detailed study of this passage see below chapter 6, under the heading "Significant Compositional Models Discovered by Schedl."

11 In the eighth instance of the formula, in verse 26, the singular form of the Greek word for "you" is used, whereas we find the plural form in the series of seven instances, which shows that this saying does not strictly belong to the series of seven.

12 The eighth instance, in verse 16 is significantly phrased differently: "Woe to you, blind guides," obviously to keep the series of seven instances of the stereotyped formula intact.

13 In 1 Cor 12:8–10, however, 9 gifts are mentioned.

Chapter 3: Clusters And Series Of Seven Divine Speeches

1 The lectures, entitled "Geloven in het spreken Gods," were published in *Rondom het Woord*, 17/4 (1975), pp. 64–81.

2 It is worth noting that verse 18, the conclusion of the narrative about Moses' stay on the mountain to hear God's instructions, originally belonged to the text of Exodus 24, where it had concluded the episode described there. At the time the Tabernacle laws were incorporated in the narrative, this verse was literally severed from its original context as a result of the application of the "split-and-insert- method" to integrate

these laws. In its present context, however, it belongs to the text of 31:12–18, as the last and seventh verse of the pericope. The fact that this literary unit has 7 verses underlines the connection between the seventh divine speech and the seventh day. Another example of such a split-and-insert operation is the way the Story of the Flood has been incorporated in the genealogy of Noah that has been split in two parts, Gen 5:32 and 9:28–29, that originally belonged together. For still another instance see below chapter 4, note 18.

3   In 32:7, 9, 33; 33:1, 5, 14, 17, 19, 20, 21; 34:1, 10, 27.

4   See below in chapter 4 the paragraph "The Primeval History in Genesis 1–11."

5   It cannot be excluded that there is a subtle reference here to the Ten Commandments. Their number does not only derive from the mnemonic function of the 10 fingers, but certainly also from the 10 Primeval Divine Utterances.

6   In chapter 5, under the heading "Examples from the book of Exodus," we shall refer to more numerical features of this text and of verses 34–38.

7   We shall pay attention to his work in chapter 6.

8   See Carol Meyers, *The Tabernacle Menorah: A Synthetic Study of a Symbol from the Biblical Cult* (Scholars Press: Missoula, MT, 1976), and her contributions "Lampstand" in *The Anchor Bible Dictionary*, vol. 4, pp. 141–143, and "Menorah" in *Theologisches Wörterbuch zum Alten Testament*, vol. IV, pp. 981–987. See also Rachel Hachlili, *The Menorah, The Ancient Seven-armed Candelabrum. Origin, Form and Significance* (Supplements to the Journal for the Study of Judaism, Volume 68), Brill, Leiden 2001 (ISBN 90 04 120173) and compare my review in *Journal for the Study of Judaism*, XXXIV, 3, pp. 323-327. Special attention deserves the study by Trudy Labuschagne, *De Menora in woord en beeld. Een studie over de vorm, functie en betekenis van de Menora in het Oude Testament en de latere symboliek* (doctorate term paper; Groningen, 1992), who has studied the relevant texts especially with regard to their literary structure and numerical aspects. She discovered significant Menorah-patterns in the Menorah passages in Exod 30:26–28; 40:17–32; 1 Chr 28:12–18; 2 Chr 13:10–11, and paid special attention to the famous Menorah- psalm, Psalm 67, and the Menorah-pattern of the seven visions in the book of Zechariah.

9   The Hebrew term can sometimes mean "before the Lord" (the rendering here given by many translations, e.g. the *Revised Standard Version* and the *Revised English Bible*), but in these two cases it has the connotation "for the face (= presence) of the Lord," "for the benefit of the Lord," i.e. for him personally.

10 See Trudy Labuschagne, *De Menora*, p. 79, to whom I owe this observation.

11 For a discussion of the problem regarding the number of visions and of the central position of the Menorah vision in the book of Zecharaiah, see Klaus Seybold, *Bilder zum Tempelbau. Die Visionen des Propheten Zacharja* (Stuttgarter Bibel Studien 70; Stuttgart, 1974), pp. 31–39, and Carol L. Meyers and Eric M. Meyers, *Haggai, Zechariah 1–8* (The Anchor Bible, vol. 25B; Garden City, NY, 1987), pp. liv-lvi and 260–277, as well as Trudy Labuschagne, *De Menora*, pp. 45–68.

12 The other series of seven stereotyped referring formulas starts in chapter 16 and ends in Num 9: 1) Lev 16:34; 2) Lev 24:23; 3) Num 1:19; 4) Num 2:33; 5) Num 3:51; 6) Num 8:3; 7) Num 8:22. In Num 3:42 we find an eighth instance, which is, however, phrased differently: "as the Lord had commanded him," obviously to keep the series of seven intact.

13 It might be a mere coincidence, but the total number of stereotyped introductory formulas in chapters 17–27 comes up to exactly 17: that is 2 (in 17–18) + 14 (in 19–25) + 1 (in 27:1, introducing the very last divine speech in Leviticus). Is this a matter of contingency, or was it purposefully designed?

14 See my book *Gods Oude Plakboek. Visie op het Oude Testament* ('s-Gravenhage, 1978; 4de druk 1990), pp. 115–117.

15 The *Revised English Bible* blurs the issue by ignoring this introductory formula.

16 See note 15 above with regard to the rendering of the Hebrew infinitive *le'mor* "saying." See below in chapter 4 note 3 in connection with this verbal form in Genesis 1:22 and 2:16.

Chapter 4: The 7+4=11 Pattern in the Pentateuch

1 These seven acts of creation do not and need not correspond with the seven days, which have their own distinct pattern.

2 The importance of *food*, the precondition for the continuation of life on earth, is stressed by the fact that a special divine decree is devoted to God's provision of food. This is corroborated by the fact that the divine command here regarding the *creation of vegetation* (1:11), being in fourth place, occupies center position. In chapter 2 we have encountered no less than *four* menorah-patterns in the New Testament with the item *food* at the center! See the paragraph "Examples from the four Gospels." The seven words of creation seem to have been an archetype for these texts.

3 The Hebrew word *le'mor*, an infinitive form, usually literally rendered "saying," means simply "as follows"; it has the same function as our quotation marks, which introduce direct speech. In both instances

this verbal form is correctly rendered, for instance, in the *Revised Standard Version*. The rendering of the *Revised English Bible* is misleading, since it suggests the use of a finite verb.

4   Gen 2:4–25 has traditionally been regarded as a second creation story. Recent research brought to light, however, that it was not really meant to be a second story of *creation* but the first phase of the Story of Adam and Eve (2:4 – 4:26), the beginning of the history of mankind, described on the basis of the primeval history of an individual male and female representing all human beings. The author deals particularly with relationship in God's creation: between God and human beings, between human beings and the earth, between humans and animals, between male and female. See my essay "Het bijbelse scheppingsgeloof in ecologisch perspectief" in *Tijdschrift voor Theologie* 30 (1990), pp. 5–17, where relevant literature is referred to.

5   For details the reader is referred to my first endeavour to chart the divine speech formulas in the Pentateuch: "The Pattern of the Divine Speech formulas in the Pentateuch," *Vetus Testamentum* 32 (1982), pp. 268–296, especially 270 and the Synopsis on pages 282ff.

6   See N. P. Bratsiotis, "Der Monolog im Alten Testament," *Zeitschrift für die Alttestamentliche Wissenschaft* 73 (1961), pp. 30–70; R. A. F. MacKenzie, "The Divine Soliloquies in Genesis," *Catholic Biblical Quarterly* 17 (1955), pp. 277–286; R. Lapointe, The Divine Monologue as a channel of Revelation," *Catholic Biblical Quarterly* 32 (1970), pp. 161–181, and see my article "The Literary and Theological Function of Divine Speech in the Pentateuch," *Congress Volume: Salamanca 1983*. Supplements to Vetus Testamentum 36 (Leiden, 1985), pp. 154–173, especially pp. 155–156.

7   There is an extra introductory formula, ᵓamarti, "I said," in verse 26!

8   H. Nobel, *Gods gedachten tellen. Numerieke structuuranalyse en de elf gedachten Gods in Genesis – 2 Koningen*, [English translation of the title: *Counting God's Thoughts. Numerical Structural Analysis and the Eleven Thoughts of God in Genesis – II Kings*], University of Groningen, published privately in 1993.

9   See my article "The Literary and Theological Function of Divine Speech in the Pentateuch," cited above in note 6, page 158.

10   For the first endeavour ever to survey and chart this complex material (without the help of the computer!) see my preliminary article "The Pattern of the Divine Speech Formulas in the Pentateuch," *Vetus Testamentum* 32 (1982), pp. 268–296 and my subsequent contribution "Additional Remarks on the Pattern of the Divine Speech Formulas in the Pentateuch," *Vetus Testamentum* 34 (1984), pp. 91–95. See also the critical remarks by Philip R. Davies and David M. Gunn,

"Pentateuchal Patterns. An examination of C. J. Labuschagne's theory," *Vetus Testamentum* 34 (1984), pp. 399–406, and my response "Pentateuchal Patterns: A Reply to P. R. Davies and D. M. Gunn," id., pp. 407–413. The verdict of Davies and Gunn, who qualified my thesis as "totally invalid," seems to have settled the matter and ended the discussion for good. Since then all was quiet on all fronts, except for a voice crying in the desert, inviting biblical scholars to address themselves to the numerical aspects of the Bible. The qualification "totally invalid," which I regard as premature and unjustified, cannot be the last word on the issue.

11 The Table of Nations in Genesis 10 has its own specific structure. See in chapter 6 the paragraph "The Rediscovery of the Numerical Architecture of the Bible by Oskar Goldberg"—the man who detected the role of the numbers 17 and 26 in Gen 10:21–32.

12 There is a *twelfth* instance of this formula: in Num 3:1. For a comprehensive study on the twelve instances see Sven Tengström, *Die Toledotformel und die literarische Struktur der priesterlichen Erweiterungsschicht im Pentateuch*. (Coniectanea Biblica, O.T. Series 17; Lund, 1981).

13 Claus Schedl, "Der brennende Dornbusch: der Kosmos als Erscheinungsbild Gottes" in A. Resch (Editor), *Kosmopathie* (Imago Mundi VIII; Innsbruck, 1981), pp. 677–711; M. Barnouin, "Recherches Numériques sur la Généalogie de Genèse V," *Revue Biblique* 77 (1970), pp. 347–365. See my article "The Life Spans of the Patriarchs," in A. S. van der Woude (editor), *New Avenues in the Study of the Old Testament* (Oudtestamentische Studiën 25; Leiden, 1989), pp. 121–127, as well as K. Th. Eisses, "Een ernstig spel met getallen. De Godsnaam in Genesis 5," *Interpretatie* (January 1996), pp. 19–21.

14 For the biblical chronology see Mordecai Cogan's contribution "Chronology" in *The Anchor Bible Dictionary*, volume I, pp. 1002–1011; K. J. Stenring, *The Enclosed Garden*, Stockholm 1966; Gerhard Larsson, *The Secret System. A Study in the Chronology of the Old Testament*, Leiden 1973; Gerhard Larsson, "Chronological Parallels Between the Creation and the Flood," *Vetus Testamentum* 27 (1977), pp. 490–492; Gerhard Larsson, "The Chronology of the Pentateuch: A Comparison of the MT and LXX," *Journal of Biblical Literature* 102 (1983), pp. 401–409; Gerhard Larsson, "The Documentary Hypothesis and the Chronological Structure of the Old Testament," *Zeitschrift für die Alttestamentliche Wissenschaft* 97 (1985), pp. 316–333; Gerhard Larsson, "Ancient Calendars Indicated in the Old Testament," *Journal for the Study of the Old Testament* 54 (1992), pp. 61–76; Gerhard Larsson, "More Quantitative Old Testament Research?" *Zeitschrift für die Alttestamentliche Wissenschaft* 110 (1998), pp. 570–580.

Other studies on the numbers in Genesis 5 are: D. V. Etz, "The Numbers of Genesis V 3–31: A Suggested Conversion and its Implications" *Vetus Testamentum* 43 (1993), pp. 171–189; D. W. Young, "On the Application of Numbers from Babylonian Mathematics to Biblical Life Spans and Epochs," *Zeitschrift für die Alttestamentliche Wissenschaft* 100 (1988), pp. 331–361; D. W. Young, "The Influence of Babylonian Algebra on Longevity among Antediluvians," *Zeitschrift für die Alttestamentliche Wissenschaft* 102 (1990), pp. 321–335, and R. Heinzerling, "Einweihung durch Henoch? Bedeutung der Altersangaben in Genesis 5," *Zeitschrift für die Alttestamentliche Wissenschaft* 110 (1999), pp. 581–589.

15 See in chapter 5 the paragraph "The Purpose of the Hidden Numerical Structures."

16 See J. Hehn, *Siebenzahl und Sabbat bei den Babyloniern und im Alten Testament* (Leipzig, 1907), especially pp. 57ff. and 77–90, and the literature cited in chapter 2 note 4 above.

17 See my commentary *Deuteronomium* (De Prediking van het Oude Testament; G. F. Callenbach, Nijkerk, 1987), volume IA and the Appendix, where the reader can find a transcription of the Hebrew text and the numerical structure analysis of Deuteronomy 1–11. This commentary is the first to offer a comprehensive numerical analysis of a complete biblical book. The remaining volumes have now all been published: volume IB (1987), volume II (1990) and volume III (1997).

18 In my view the introduction in 4:44–49, which is remarkably similar to the introduction in 1:1–5, originally belonged to the text of 1:1 – 3:29 as an epilogue. When chapter 4:1–43 was incorporated by means of the "split-and-insert" technique, the epilogue was transferred to its present place—see my *Deuteronomium*, volume IA, pp. 49–50. For more examples of this technique see chapter 3 note 2.

19 For particulars see the table of contents in my commentary, volume IA, pp. 7–10 and 49–50.

Chapter 5: The Secret of the Hidden Sacred Numbers 17 and 26

1 In such an analysis, which should be done by a mathematician, the frequency of occurrence of the divine name numbers and their multiples could be compared with that of 16, 19, 25 and 27 and their multiples. For an initial attempt to do this, see Rüdiger Heinzerling's Homepage, *http://home.t-online.de/home/Ruediger.Heinzerling/*, entitled "Kurze Einführung in die quantitative Strukturanalyse (QSA) biblischer Texte." Heinzerling offers an introduction to Numerical Structural Analysis, for which he uses the term "Quantitative Struc-

tural Analysis," maintaining that this type of text analysis cannot dispense with statistics.

2   See the following articles: "The Literary and Theological Function of Divine Speech in the Pentateuch," in *Congress Volume: Salamanca 1983* (Supplements to Vetus Testamentum 36; Leiden: E. J. Brill, 1985), pp. 154–173; "Divine Speech in Deuteronomy," in Norbert Lohfink (editor), *Das Deuteronomium. Entstehung, Gestalt und Botschaft.* (Bibliotheca Ephemeridum Theologicarum Lovaniensium 68; Leuven, 1985), pp. 111–126; and "Neue Wege und Perspektiven in der Pentateuchforschung," *Vetus Testamentum* 36 (1986), pp. 146–162.

3   For a more comprehensive analysis of Exod 3:1 – 4:17 see my contribution cited above in chapter 1 note 1.

4   This passage, together with the other Amalek passages, has recently been studied, with due regard for their numerical aspects, by Auke Schuil in his dissertation *Amalek. Onderzoek naar oorsprong en ontwikkeling van Amaleks rol in het Oude Testament* (Zoetermeer: Uitgeverij Boekencentrum, 1997).

5   For a more extensive survey covering the books of Leviticus and Numbers as well, see my 1985 article on divine speech in the Pentateuch, cited above in note 2, especially pp. 162–167.

6   These instances are 7:4; 11:13–15; 17:3; 28:20 and 29:5–6—see my Deuteronomy commentary, volume IB, 108. In some translations the first person form is changed into third person—see the note in the *Revised Standard Version* at Deut 11:15.

7   For an exposition of the idea of divine speech as a literary technique used to express a religious conviction, the reader with a command of Dutch is referred to my article "Geloven in het spreken Gods" cited above in chapter 3 note 1, and to my book *Zin en onzin rond de Bijbel*, chapter 6, available on my website: www.labuschagne.nl.

8   The total number of words depend upon my view of the delimiting of the divine speech in chapter 32. For particulars see my contribution "Divine Speech in Deuteronomy," in Norbert Lohfink (editor), *Das Deuteronomium: Entstehung, Gestalt und Botschaft* (Bibliotheca Ephemeridum Theologicarum Lovaniensium 68; Leuven, 1985), pp. 111–126, and my article "Neue Wege und Perspektiven in der Pentateuchforschung," *Vetus Testamentum* 36 (1986), pp. 146–173, especially p. 156.

9   We shall have a closer look at these chapters below under "Counting verses in Deuteronomy." For more examples of series of 10 see chapter 6 under "Significant Compositional Models Discovered by Schedl."

10 In three texts the exact length of the phrase is problematic. In 26:16 the phrase in my view has 5 Hebrew words [but it might have 11]: "this day the Lord your God commands you [to do these statutes and ordinances]" and in 28:69 (29:1) the phrase consists of 5 words in my view [but it might consist of 11 words]: "which the Lord commanded Moses [to make with the people of Israel in Moab]." In 13:6(5) I regard the phrase to be "in which the Lord commanded you to walk" (6 words).

11 See my commentary, volume III, page 13.

12 Significantly enough every one of these four sets of laws contains a marriage law, namely that in 21:10–14 for set 6, those in 22:13–29 for set 7, that in 23:1 (22:30) for set 8, and that in 24:1–4 for set 9. The tenth set has its marriage law in 25:5–10.

13 See my commentary, volume III, 165–168, and especially my contribution "The Setting of the Song of Moses in Deuteronomy," in *Deuteronomy and Deuteronomic Literature*. Festschrift C. H. W. Brekelmans, edited by M. Vervenne and J. Lust (Bibliotheca Ephemeridum Theologicarum Lovaniensium 133; Leuven: Leuven University Press / Uitgeverij Peeters, 1997), pp. 111–129.

14 In his letter of 17 May 1986 he wrote: "[Ich] habe Ihre Artikel wieder durchgelesen! Das auffallendste daran ist wohl, dass sich aus der streng durchgeführten Textstruktur Zahlen ergeben, die auf einen Gottesnamen weisen." Referring to Scholem's remarks about the Jewish tradition that the name of God was interwoven in the text of the Torah, he went on: "Wäre es nicht möglich, dass in der späteren mittelalterlichen Kabbala noch das Wissen davon erhalten war, dass der biblische Text tatsächlich nach der Zahlen des Gottesnamens durchkomponiert wurde???!!!."

15 See above chapter 1 note 3 and the passage preceding it.

16 For the *Sepher ha-Temunah* see Gershom Scholem, *Major Trends in Jewish Mysticism* (New York 1961), pp. 136–137. In his book *Ursprung und Anfänge der Kabbala* (Berlin, 1962), pp. 414–415, he writes: "Der Name Gottes ist eben auf mystische Weise überall in der Torah enthalten und, wie später zum Beispiel Gikatilla sagt, in sie eingewoben." See also his book *Zur Kabbala und ihrer Symbolik* (Frankfurt, 1973), p. 69, where he writes: "Es scheint dass Gikatilla als erster diesen Begriff des Gewebes (*'ariga*) benutzte, um zu beschreiben, wie der Name Gottes in der Textur der Tora immer wieder vorkommt." In the *Encyclopaedia Judaica*, volume 15 (1971), p. 1241, we read "Some said the entire Torah consists of the name of God set in succession . . . or interwoven in a fabric . . ."

17 See Claus Schedl, *Baupläne des Wortes: Einführung in die biblische Logotechnik* (Vienna, 1974), p. 22.

18 The title of the original Dutch edition of this book, *Vertellen met getallen*, is based upon this observation. It means "recounting by numbers," or "recounting by counting."

19 See my article on divine speech in the Pentateuch cited above, pages 172–173, and my commentary, volume IA page 48 and the note on page 299, as well as volume III, pages 132–134.

20 See Gerrit Ruiterkamp, *Gezegend ben je! Een studie van achtergrond, vorm en functie van de Aäronitische zegen (Numeri 6:22–27)*, Faculteit der Godgeleerdheid, Rijksuniversiteit te Groningen 1988, who has shown how this passage is structured around the divine name numbers 17 and 26 and the number 33, the numerical value of *brk*, "to bless." Incidentally the thirty-third word in the text is the word *shalom*, "peace."

21 This is in line with what is said in Exod 20:24b: "In every place where I cause my name to be invoked, I will come to you and bless you." Compare the words of Jesus in Matt 18:20 "Where two or three are gathered in my name, there am I in the midst of them."

22 See my article "The Life Spans of the Patriarchs," cited above in chapter 4 note 13.

23 Nahum Sarna, *Understanding Genesis* (The Jewish Theological Seminary of America: New York, 1966), pp. 83–85; Stanley Gevirtz, "The Life Spans of Joseph and Enoch and the Parallelism *šib'tayim - šib'im - wešib'ah*," *Journal of Biblical Literature* 96 (1977), pp. 570–571.

24 James G. Williams, "Number Symbolism and Joseph as the Symbol of Completion," *Journal of Biblical Literature* 98 (1979), pp. 86–87.

25 Duane Christensen, "Did People Live to be Hundreds of Years Old Before the Flood?," *The Genesis Debate*, ed. Ronald Youngblood (Nelson: Nashville, 1986), pp. 166–183.

26 *Pentateuch with Rashi's Commentary* (ed. A. M. Silberman; London: Shapiro, Vallentine, 1946), p. 130.

27 *Pentateuch* (ed. Silberman), p. 130.

28 See Hans A. Hutmacher, *Symbolik der biblischen Zahlen und Zeiten* (Paderborn-München-Wien-Zürich, 1993), p. 52.

29 Duane Christensen, *Bible 101: God's Story in Human History* (BIBAL Press: N. Richland Hills, TX, 1997), pp. 59–60.

30 See Duane L. Christensen (Editor), *A Song of Power and the Power of Song: Essays on the Book of Deuteronomy*, Winona Lake, IN, 1993, p. 17 note 19. See also his remarks in his article, "Biblical Genealogies and Eschatological Speculation," *Perspectives in Religious Studies* 14 (1987),

pp. 59–65; and "Josephus and the Twenty-Two-Book Canon of Sacred Scripture," *Journal of the Evangelical Theological Society* 29 (1986), pp. 37–46. See my article "The Setting of the Song of Moses in Deuteronomy" (1997), p. 119, cited in note 13 above.

31 For particulars the reader is referred to my commentary, volume IA, 154–155, 161–163, where I adduced evidence to this effect with respect to the insertion of the so-called ethnographic notices in 2:10–12 and 2:20–23. See also volume III, 12–15, 19–21 and the chapter dealing with the redaction history of the book, pages 337–360, and particularly my article "The Setting of the Song of Moses in Deuteronomy," cited in note 13 above.

Chapter 6: The Bible as a High-Grade Literary Work Of Art

1 L. Alonso-Schökel, *Das Alte Testament als literarisches Kunstwerk* (Köln, 1971); W. Richter, *Exegese als Literaturwissenschaft. Entwurf einer alttestamentlichen Literaturtheorie und Methodologie* (Göttingen, 1971); M. Weiss, *The Bible From Within. The Method of Total Interpretation* (Jerusalem, 1984); J. Muilenburg, "Form Criticism and Beyond," *Journal of Biblical Literature*, 88 (1969), pp. 1–18. See also J. J. Jackson and M. Kessler, *Rhetorical Criticism. Essays in Honor of James Muilenburg* (Pittsburg, 1974). For a handsome introduction to the "Amsterdam-School" see M. Kessler, *Voices from Amsterdam: A Modern Tradition of Reading Biblical Narrative* (The Society of Biblical Literature Semeia Studies; Atlanta: Scholars Press, 1994); and for a critical evaluation and methodological reflection see R. Oost, *Omstreden Bijbeluitleg: Aspecten en achtergronden van de hermeneutische discussie rondom de exegese van het Oude Testament in Nederland. Een bijdrage tot een gesprek* (Groningen dissertation; J. H. Kok, Kampen 1986; 2nd print 1987). A related "school" is the "Sheffield School"—see D. J. A. Clines, D. M. Gunn and A. J. Hauser (editors), *Art and Meaning: Rhetoric in Biblical Literature* (Sheffield, 1982). Worth mentioning are the publications by J. P. Fokkelman, for instance, *Narrative Art in Genesis. Specimens of Stylistic and Structural Analysis*, (Assen/Amsterdam, 1975), and *Narrative Art and Poetry in the Books of Samuel*, Volume I-IV, (Assen, 1981–1993).

2 For a detailed discussion and a plea for the integration of numerical structural analysis in literary criticism, see my article "De literairkritische methode," cited above in chapter 1 note 1.

3 See J. M. Oesch, *Petucha und Setuma*. (Orbis biblicus et Orientalis 27; Fribourg, 1977), and his article "Textgliederung im Alten Testament und in den Qumranhandschriften," *Henoch* 5 (1983), pp. 289–321. See also R. Wonneberger, *Leitfaden zur Biblia Hebraica* (Göttingen, 1984), pp. 18–19. Some writers on biblical subjects, for instance, M. van Tijn en D.

Nicolai in their book *Belofte en Catastrofe* (Bloemendaal, 1977), p. 23, assert that the Masoretes had no notion whatsoever of the division of the text in pericopes. However, such a claim has no foundation, neither is there any justification for their disregard of the masoretic divisions in favor of their own subjective delimitations. Moreover, the way they treat the text in search of "central phrases," "key words" and "the central core," which they believe can be found in every text and must be found at all costs, is questionable. Such a search is of course legitimate, but it has its limits. Though many texts do have a structural (even mathematical) center, as I have demonstrated above, most texts do not.

4   The only problem seems to be the open space after Gen 44:17, which is indicated in *Biblia Hebraica Stuttgartensia* and in Rudolph Kittel's *Biblia Hebraica* for some reason or other as a *parashah petuchah*, but appears to be a *parashah setumah* in *Codex Leningrad* (open space at the beginning of the line—see H. Nobel, *Gods gedachten tellen*, p. 130, note 33 and p. 132, note 43). However, the half open line could be regarded as an error in the codex, since the caesura is a strong one, also marking the beginning of both a *Seder* in the Palestinian reading cycle and a *Parash* in the Babylonian cycle. I have not been able to check other medieval manuscripts on this point, which are usually in agreement with *Codex Leningrad*. If the *parashah setumah* space is not an error, the total number of sub-sections would be 42 instead of 43.

5   Oskar Goldberg, *Die fünf Bücher Mosis ein Zahlengebäude: Die Feststellung einer einheitlich durchgeführten Zahlenschrift* [*The Five Books of Moses an Architecture of Numbers: The Observation of a Consistently Executed Writing-in-Numbers*] (Berlin, 1908). It was Claus Schedl who drew my attention to this book.

6   After the second world war a series of four articles by Goldberg, entitled "Das Zahlengebäude des Pentateuch: Eine Geheimschrift in den fünf Büchern Moses," were published in *La Revue Juive* numbers 89–93 (1947), pages 13–22; 100–105; 142–149; 193–199, in which he repeated his 1908 thesis, substantiating it with more examples. A French version appeared in numbers 94–95. In his opinion the qualification "Zahlengebäude" applies only to the Pentateuch, clearly due to the lack of research outside the Pentateuch—see his explicit remark in the last article of the 1947 series, p. 198: "Die heilige Zahlen kommen systematisch nur im Pentateuch vor . . ."

7   Hans A. Hutmacher's *Symbolik der biblischen Zahlen und Zeiten*, (Paderborn-München-Wien-Zürich, 1993), the most recent book written in the same vein as Goldbergs mathematical kabbalistic exercises, is strictly about number symbolism and does not contribute anything to a better understanding of the biblical text and its numerical

structure. See the review by Karl Prenner in *Theologie der Gegenwart*, 37 (1994), pp. 155–157.

8   Schedl's pioneering work is his *Baupläne des Wortes. Einführung in die biblische Logotechnik* (Wien, 1974). Twenty-two of his earlier articles and books, published during the sixties and early seventies, are listed on pages 30–31 of this book. Other major works on the Old Testament are: *Rufer des Heils in heilloser Zeit. Der Prophet Jesajah Kapitel I-XII logotechnisch und bibeltheologisch erklärt* (Paderborn, 1973), and *Zur Theologie des Alten Testaments. Der göttliche Sprachvorgang in Schöpfung und Geschichte* (Paderborn, 1986). Two books deal specifically with the New Testament: *Als sich der Pfingsttag erfüllte. Erklärung der Pfingstperikope Apg. 2,1–47* (Wien-Freiburg-Basel, 1982), and *Zur Christologie der Evangelien* (Wien-Freiburg-Basel, 1984).

9   See Claus Schedl, *Als sich der Pfingsttag erfüllte. Erklärung der Pfingstperikope Apg 2,1–47* (Wien-Freiburg-Basel, 1982), pp. 17–20.

10 See his *Baupläne des Wortes*, pp. 18–21, for his critical remarks with regard to the current methods and see also my article cited in chapter 1 note 1.

11 See his book *Talmud, Evangelium, Synagoge* (Innsbruck-Wien-München, 1969), a study of the Talmud-tractate *Aboth*, "Fathers," some chapters from the Gospel of Matthew, and a number of liturgical texts for the synagogue. He considered the study of early Jewish literature indispensable for biblical scholars. At the 1965 meeting of the International Organisation for the Study of the Old Testament in Geneva he expressed this conviction in the following way: "Before we follow Wellhausen and his sons in Source Criticism, we should go and sit at the feet of Rabbi Akibah or Rabbi Gamaliel and study their way of studying Scripture . . ."

12 See his *Baupläne des Wortes*, pp. 44–47. For an introduction to the *Sefer Jetzirah* see Gershom Scholem, *Kabbalah* (Jerusalem, 1974), pp. 21–30, and especially Aryeh Kaplan, *Sefer Yetzirah: The Book of Creation* (York Beach, Maine, 1990).

13 See also Num 8:4; Acts 7:44 and Heb 8:5.

14 See his dissertation *Gods gedachten tellen*, cited above in chapter 4 note 8, especially pages 29–46.

15 See my critical review of Menken's dissertation in my 1987 article cited above, pages 1–16; M. J. J. Menken, *Numerical Literary Techniques in John. The Fourth Evangelist's Use of Numbers of Words and Syllables* (Supplements to Novum Testamentum 15; Leiden, 1985). For Smit Sibinga's most important publications see my article page 12.

16 See Claus Schedl, *Baupläne*, p. 51, and M. J. J. Menken, *Numerical Techniques*, pp. 28 and 39.

17 See the critical remarks by H. Nobel, *Gods gedachten tellen*, pp. 39–46, especially 42–43.

18 See chapter 5 under the heading "The symbolic meaning of 17 and 26."

19 Dr. R. Oost, who has directed my attention to the mathematical center of the psalm, and Jacob Bazak have independently observed this center. Bazak has discovered such centers in Psalm 34, 81 and 92 as well. See Jacob Bazak, "Numerical Devices in Biblical Poetry," *Vetus Testamentum* 38 (1988), pp. 333–337.

20 See my commentary volume I, p. 96 and III, pp. 222–229, and for further examples see the register in volume III, p. 390, as well as the four appendixes.

21 See in this respect above chapter 2 under the heading "Examples from the Four Gospels," where I have mentioned seven instances of texts emphasizing the importance of food.

22 See my commentary, volume IA, pp. 34–35, where the instances occurring in chapters 1–11 are cited, and volume II, pp. 79–90, 132–133, 161, and 187, for those in chapters 12–26.

23 See chapter 2 of Duane Christensen's book *Bible 101* (Richland Hills, TX: BIBAL Press, 1997), pp. 15–66.

24 See Duane Christensen, "Josephus and the Twenty-two-book Canon of Sacred Scripture," *Journal of the Evangelical Theological Society* 29/1 (March 1986), pp. 37–46.

25 See Claus Schedl, *Baupläne*, p. 172.

26 For some New Testament instances see, M. J. J. Menken, *Numerical Literary Techniques in John* (cited above in note 15), pp. 18, 49, 55, 64, 83–84, 146, 251, and 253.

27 See my commentary, volume IA, pp. 211–213 for the other numerical features.

28 For its numerical aspects see my commentary, pages 267–268.

29 For a detailed analysis of Psalm 79 see my contribution "On the Structural Use of Numbers as a Compositional Technique," *Journal of Northwest Semitic Languages* 12 (1984 [1986]), pp. 87–99, incidentally the first psalm I analysed logotechnically.

30 For a detailed discussion of Zech 4:1–14, particularly with regard to its numerical aspects, see the study on the Menorah by Trudy Labuschagne (cited above in chapter 3 note 8), pp. 45–68, especially

45–52. She drew my attention to the numerical value of the name Zerubbabel.

31 See my commentary, volume IA, pp.154–155, and the Appendix, page 14.

32 See M. J. J. Menken, *Numerical Literary Techniques in John*, pp. 108–110, and compare 272, where more examples are mentioned.

33 Dr. H. Nobel has pointed this out to me in a private communication.

34 I got the information about Christensen's view of the structure of Qohelet in a private communication from him, but see now his book *Bible 104—the Writings: a Study Guide* (Richland Hills, TX: BIBAL Press, 1998), pp. 87–91.

Chapter 7: Proper Use and Misuse of Numbers

1 See H. D. A. Mayes, *Deuteronomy*. The New Century Bible Commentary (Grand Rapids, 1981), pp. 191–193.

2 For this interpretation of the psalm see my book *The Incomparability of Yahweh in the Old Testament* (Leiden, 1966), pp. 83–85, and compare M. Dahood, *Psalms II*. Anchor Bible (New York, 1968), pp. 268–271. See for the meaning of ʾ*amarti*, "I thought," my article "Some remarks on the translation and meaning of ʾ*amarti* in the Psalms" in *New Light on Some Old Testament Problems* (Papers read at fifth meeting [of the Outestamentiese Werkgemeenskap in Suid-Afrika] Held at the University of South Africa, Pretoria 30 January–2 February 1962), pp. 27–33.

3 For the different numerical values of *kbd/kbwd*, "glory," see chapter 5 under "The Symbolic Meaning of 17 and 26."

4 For a discussion of the structure of Psalm 8 see Meir Weiss, *The Bible From Within: The Method of Total Interpretation* (Jerusalem, 1984), pp. 293–297, and Eep Talstra, "Singers and Syntax: On the Balance of Grammar and Poetry in Psalm 8," in Janet Dyk (editor), *Give Ear to My Words: Psalms and other Poetry in and around the Hebrew Bible:* Essays in honor of Professor N. A. van Uchelen (Amsterdam, 1996), pp. 11–22.

5 See chapter 5 under "The Divine Name Interwoven in the Fabric of the Text."

6 See the open space in the middle of 9:1 in the *Revised English Bible*.

7 The following examples I found in George Ifrah's book *De wereld van het getal*, Katwijk aan Zee 1988, 219–221 (original French title: *Les Chiffres ou L'histoire d'une grande invention* (Paris, 1985); English translation: *From One to Zero*), and in John Allen Paulos's booklet (pp. 86–87), cited in chapter 1 note 7.

8   David Wells, *The Penguin Dictionary of Curious and Interesting Numbers* (London, 1986), p. 124. That the name Shakespeare is really spelled differently does not seem to be a problem.

9   I refer to press reports, for instance in *Nachrichten aus Israel* [English version: *Dispatch from Jerusalem*], Nr. 4 (1986) about the "findings," based upon the technique of equidistant letter sequences, by M. Katz and F. Weiner, the "codes" computed by rabbi D. Ordman, who claimed to have proved by computer the existence of God, and the most recent "codes" invented by Michael Drosnin, published as *The Bible Code* (New York, 1997).

10   See chapter 6 under "The Numerical Architecture of the Hebrew Bible Rediscovered" and Goldberg's articles in *La Revue Juive* (cited there in note 6), especially pages 15–17 and 199.

11   I could trace the following titles of Panin's publications, with difficulty, since it concerns mostly obscure and amateurish publishers: *Numeric Greek New Testament*; *Numeric English New Testament*; and *The Bible—a Mathematical Challenge*. Some of his work has been published by F. W. Grant, *Numerical Bible* (7 volumes), and *Numerical Structure of Scripture*; and by K. L. Brooks, *Overwhelming Mathematical Evidence of the Divine Inspiration of the Scriptures from the Works of Dr. Ivan Panin, Harvard Scholar and Mathematician*. The Southwest Radio Church of the Air, in Oklahoma City, has published some of his lectures: *Astounding New Discoveries*. Panin's disciple, K. G. Sabiers, a member of "The International Church of the Foursquare Gospel" wrote a book in the early forties about the ideas of his master: *Astonishing New Discoveries: Thousands of Amazing Facts Discovered Beneath the Very Surface of the Bible Text*, which was translated into German and reprinted several times: *Erstaunliche neue Entdeckungen. Wissenschaft beweist: Die Bibel ist wörtlich von Gott inspiriert*, Heijkoop Verlag, Schwelm 1975 (8th reprint). This book was subjected to a serious, and devastating, review by Heinrich & Peter von Siebenthal, in three articles in which the authors unmasked the "discoveries" as unsound and flimsy, recommending not to read the book: (1) "Im Bibeltext verborgene Zahlenkombinationen als Beweis der göttlichen Inspiration?," *Fundamentum* (Erstausgabe, Basle 1980), pp. 35–52; (2) idem, *Fundamentum* (Heft 1/1981), pp. 30–47; (3) idem, *Fundamentum* (Erstausgabe, 2. Auflage 1984), pp. 35–52. I might mention two further books written in Sabiers's vein: O.T. Allis, *Bible Numerics* (Chicago: Moody Press, 1944; reprinted by the Presbyterian and Reformed Publishing Co., Nutley, N. J. 1974); and W. E. Filmer has written a booklet, *God Counts. A Study in Bible Numbers* (Croydon, 1947). The Association of the Covenant People, in Burnabay, Canada, published *The Shorter Works of Ivan Panin*. Claus Schedl sent me a copy of an article in a missionary journal entitled "*Prof. Panins wissenschaftlicher Beweis:*

Die Bibel ist nicht Menschenwerk. 'Wasserzeichen' bürgt für Echtheit— Zahlengeheimschlüssel löst alle Fragen."

12 This applies to the investigations by Peter Friesenhahn as well, whose dissertation, *Hellenistische Wortzahlenmystik im Neuen Testament* (Leipzig/Berlin, 1935; republished by Verlag B. R. Grüner in Amsterdam in 1970), has not received the attention it deserves.

13 An "Academie voor de Hebreeuwse Bijbel en de Hebreeuwse Taal" was established to make his kabbalistic ideas public through courses and pamphlets. His major work was published in 1963: *De Bijbel als Schepping*, translated into German: *Der Göttliche Bauplan der Welt*, 1966, followed by *Die Rolle Esther; das Buch Esther nach der ältesten jüdischen Überlieferung* (Zürich, 1968). A fascinating biography of Weinreb was published in 1997 by Regina Grüter, *Een fantast schrijft geschiedenis. De affaires rond Friedrich Weinreb*, Uitgeverij Balans.

About the Author

Casper Labuschagne was born in Heilbron, South Africa in 1929. He studied Semitic languages and theology at the University of Pretoria and at the State University in Groningen, The Netherlands, from 1947 to 1956. He holds an M.A. in Semitic languages and a Doctor of Divinity from the University of Pretoria. He was a minister of the Dutch Reformed Church in South Africa in 1957 and 1958. He was a senior lecturer in Semitic languages at the University of Pretoria and from 1967 to his retirement in 1991, was lecturer and later professor of Old Testament at the State University in Groningen. He has published a major, four-volume commentary on Deuteronomy in Dutch.

His magnum opus is his quantitative structural analysis of the Psalms and the books of Genesis through Malachi, published on the internet.

The pdf files are downloadable for free. Go to www.labuschagne.nl.

Index of Scripture Citations

Hebrew Bible

Genesis

Chapter 1	41, 46-47, 57, 60, 62
1:1 - 2:3	26, 57, 108, 110
1:1-5	110
1:1-25	59
1:3	53, 58, 162
1:5	61
1:6	53, 58
1:6-8	110
1:8	61
1:9	53, 58
1:9-13	110
1:10	61
1:11	53, 58, 169
1:14	53, 58
1:14-19	110
1:20	53, 58
1:20-23	110
1:22	58, 169
1:24	53, 58
1:24-31	110
1:26 - 2:25	78
1:26	53, 58-59, 63, 76
1:26-30	59
1:28	53, 58-59, 70
1:29	53, 58
1:31	45
Chapters 1-2	58, 62, 78
Chapters 1-11	36, 57, 64, 77-78
Chapter 2	108
2:1-3	110
2:3	45, 108
2:4 - 3:21	110
2:4 - 3:24	108
2:4 - 4:26	57, 60, 170
2:4 - 10:32	110
2:4	66, 108-109
2:4-25	108, 170

Genesis (cont.)

2:7	60
2:16	58, 169
2:18	58-60, 63, 76
Chapter 3	42, 60, 78
3:1	60
3:3	60
3:9	53, 61
3:11	53, 61
3:13	53, 61
3:14	53, 61
3:16	53, 61
3:17	53, 60-61
3:20	60
3:22 - 4:26	110
3:22	53, 61, 63, 76
Chapters 3-4	60, 62, 78
Chapter 4	26, 57, 60, 78
4:1-22	64-65
4:2	55
4:3	55
4:4-5	55
4:6	55, 61
4:7-9	55
4:9	61
4:10	55, 61
4:11-12	55
4:13	55
4:14-17	55
4:15	61
Chapter 5	57, 61, 67, 172
5:1	66
5:1-20	110
5:1-32	64-65
5:2	61
5:21-24	110
5:25-27	110
5:28 - 6:4	110
5:32	168
Chapters 5-11	57
6:3 - 9:7	61-62

Genesis (cont.)

6:3	53, 62-63, 67-68, 76
6:5-8	110
6:7	53, 62-63, 76
6:9 - 9:17	110
6:9	66
6:13	53, 62
Chapters 6-9	42, 53, 57, 61
Chapters 6-11	62
Chapter 7	27
7:1	53, 62
7:2	27
7:3	27
7:15	53
7:21	53
8:15	62
8:21	62-63
8:21-22	63, 76
9:1	53, 62
9:8 - 11:9	78
9:8	53, 62
9:8-17	61
9:12	53, 62
9:17	53, 62
9:18-29	110
9:28-29	168
Chapter 10	57, 102, 171
10:1	66
10:1-32	110
10:21-32	103, 111, 171
Chapter 11	102
11:1 - 25:18	110
11:1-9	71, 110
11:6	62
11:6-7	62-63, 76
11:8	71
11:10 - 12:9	110
11:10	66
11:10-27	64-65
11:10-32	67

Index of Scripture Citations

Genesis (cont.)

11:27 - 25:11	66
11:27	66, 109
12:1	109
12:10 - 13:18	110
Chapters 12-50	71
14:1 - 17:27	110
Chapter 15	42
15:1	53
15:1-16	53-54
15:4	53
15:5	53, 62
15:7	53
15:9	53
15:13	53
15:17-21	54
16:11-12	78
Chapter 17	42
Chapter 18	42, 63
18:1 - 21:21	110
18:17-19	63, 77
Chapters 20-24	78
21:17-18	78
21:22-34	110
21:28-29	29
Chapter 22	42
22:1-19	110
22:20 - 24:67	110
25:1-11	66
25:1-18	110
25:7-11	102
25:12	66
25:12-18	66
25:19 - 32:3	110
25:19 - 36:43	110
25:19	66-67
25:23	78
Chapters 25-28	78
Chapters 25-31	78
26:2-5	78
27:40	8
28:13-15	78
Chapter 30	28
30:25	100
Chapter 31	42
31:3	53, 57, 78
31:11	53, 57

Genesis (cont.)

31:11-13	78
31:12	53, 57
31:24	53, 57, 78
31:29	53, 57, 78
Chapters 31-32	53, 57
32:4 - 34:31	110
32:10	53, 57
32:10-13	78
32:13	53, 57
32:27	53, 57
32:28	53, 57
32:29	53, 57
32:30	53, 57
Chapter 33	27
Chapter 35	42
35:1	53
35:1-8	110
35:9-22	110
35:10	53
35:10-12	78
35:11	53
35:23-29	110
Chapters 35-48	53
36:1	66
36:1-30	110
36:9	66
36:31-43	110
37:1 - 50:26	110
37:1-36	110
37:2	66, 102
38:1 - 40:23	110
41:1 - 44:17	110
44:17	177
44:18 - 46:27	110
46:2	53
46:3	53
46:3-4	78
46:28 - 47:31	110
47:9	100
47:28	102
48:1-22	110
48:4	53
49:1-4	110
49:5-12	110
49:13-26	110
49:27 - 50:26	110

Exodus

2:1-25	79
Chapter 3	63
3:1 - 4:17	79, 173
3:1-22	79
3:4	61
3:14	97
3:16	79
3:17	63, 77, 79
3:18	79
3:21-22	79
Chapters 3-4	42
4:1-17	53-54, 79, 83
4:2	53
4:3	53
4:4	53
4:6	53
4:7	53
4:11	53
4:14	53
6:14	50
7:1	50
Chapter 11	50
Chapter 13	63
13:17	63, 77
14:15-19	137-138
14:19	138
15:1-20	80
15:25-26	80
17:1-7	81
17:5-6	81
17:8-16	81, 111-112
Chapter 19	42
19:3	61
19:3-8	81
Chapter 20	81
20:1-17	81
20:7	81
20:11	81
20:24	175
22:27	9
23:20-23	137
23:21	138
23:23	138
Chapter 24	167
24:16	61
25:1 - 30:10	42-43

Index of Scripture Citations

Exodus (cont.)		Exodus (cont.)		Leviticus (cont.)	
25:1	42	Chapters 35-40	42, 44	6:17	50
25:9	118	36:1	44	6:19	50
25:37	29	36:5	44	6:24	50
25:40	118	38:22	44	7:22	50
Chapters 25-31	42-44	Chapter 39	42, 46	7:28	50
Chapters 25-40	42,44	39:1	45	Chapters 7-8	50
30:11 - 31:17	42, 50	39:1-31	45	8:1	50
30:11-16	43	39:5	45	8:3	51
30:17-21	43	39:7	45	8:8	9
30:22-33	43, 48	39:21	45	8:9	51
30:26-28	48, 168	39:26	45	8:11	29
30:34-38	43	39:29	45	8:13	51
Chapters 30-31	42	39:31	45	8:17	51
31:1-11	43	39:32	46	8:21	51
31:12-17	43, 45, 52	39:32-43	45	8:29	51
31:12-18	168	39:42	46	8:36	51
31:17	44	39:43	43, 45-46	9:7	51
31:18	167	Chapters 39-40	51	9:10	51
32:7	168	Chapter 40	42	Chapters 9-10	51
32:9	168	40:1	44	10:8	50
32:33	168	40:1-16	46	10:8-11	50
Chapters 32-34	42,44	40:16	46	10:12-20	50
Chapters 32-40	44	40:17-32	168	10:15	51
33:1	168	40:17-33	46, 81-82	10:16	9
33:1-3	137-138	40:17-38	81	11:1	51
33:2	138	40:19	46	11:42	9
33:5	168	40:21	46	Chapters 11-16	51
33:14	168	40:23	46-47	12:1	51
33:17	168	40:25	46-47	13:1	51
33:17-23	90	40:27	46	14:1	51
33:19	168	40:29	46	14:33	51
33:20	168	40:32	46	15:1	51
33:21	168	40:34-35	82	15:7	9
33:21-22	91	40:34-38	81, 168	15:19	28
33:21-23	91	40:36-38	82	15:28	28
33:23	91			Chapter 16	169
33:34	138	**Leviticus**		16:1	51
34:1	168	1:1	50, 61	16:2	51
34:10	168	1:6	50	16:34	51, 169
34:27	168	Chapters 1-10	50	17:10-14	80
Chapter 35	42	4:1	50	Chapters 17-18	51, 169
35:1	44	4:6	29		
35:1-3	45	5:14	50	Chapters 17-26	51
35:4	44	5:20	50	Chapter 19	52
35:10	44	6:1	50	19:1	52
35:29	44-45	6:8	50	Chapters 19-23	52
Chapters 35-38	44	6:12	50	Chapters 19-25	169

Leviticus (cont.)		Deuteronomy		Deuteronomy (cont.)	
Chapters 19-26	52	1:1 - 3:29	172	2:9-13	73
20:1	52	1:1	72	2:10-12	136, 176
21:1	52	1:1-5	136, 172	2:15	72
21:16	52	1:5	72	2:16 - 3:29	73
22:1	52	1:6 - 4:40	85	2:16	72
22:17	52	1:6	72	2:18-25	73
22:26	52	1:8	72	2:19	72
23:1	52	1:9	72	2:20	72
23:8	52	1:9-11	124	2:20-23	176
23:9	52	1:9-14	124	2:23	72
23:23	52	1:12-14	124	2:24	72
23:26	52	1:15	72	2:25	72
23:33	52	1:16	72	2:26	72
24:1	52	1:18	72	2:30	72
24:13	52	1:19	72	2:31	72
24:23	169	1:19-22	73	2:35	72
Chapter 25	28	1:22	72	2:36	72
25:1	52	1:23	72	2:37	72
Chapter 26	27	1:28	72	3:1	72-73
26:18	27	1:29	72	3:1-2	129
26:21	27	1:33	72	3:1-7	73
26:24	27	1:34	72, 131	3:2	73
26:28	27	1:34-40	131	3:3-4	129
27:1	169	1:35	131	3:3-7	73
		1:36	131	3:4	72
		1:37	131	3:5	72
Numbers		1:38	131	3:7	72
1:19	169	1:39	131	3:8	72
2:33	169	1:40	72, 131	3:8-10	129
3:1	171	1:41	72	3:10	72
3:42	169	1:45	72	3:11	72
3:51	169	1:46	72	3:14	72
6:27	97	Chapters 1-3	71, 73,	3:15	72
8:1	29		83-84, 86	3:17	72
8:3	169	Chapters 1-11	71, 84,	3:18	72
8:4	178		172, 179	3:18-20	73
8:22	169	Chapters 1-34	83	3:20	72
Chapter 9	169	2:1	72	3:21	72
Chapter 11	28	2:2	72	3:22	72
17:20	9	2:2-6	73	3:23	72
19:11	28	2:2-13	73	3:23-29	73, 132
19:14	28	2:7	73	3:25	72
19:16	28	2:8	72	3:26	72, 132
23:1	29	2:8-15	136	3:26-28	73

Index of Scripture Citations

Deuteronomy (cont.)		Deuteronomy (cont.)		Deuteronomy (cont.)	
3:29	72	Chapters 12-34	84	29:19-20	128
Chapter 4	86	13:6	174	29:28	95
4:1-43	71, 86, 133, 172	14:1-21	87	30:1-2	129
		14:22 - 16:17	87	30:29-30	129
4:5-8	128	15:4-6	137	Chapter 31	124
4:20-2	132	16:1-4	137	31:1-13	87
4:20-24	132	16:10-11	128	31:2-6	85
4:22	132	16:18 - 18:22	87	31:7-8	85
4:32-35	128	17: 16-17	137	31:14 - 34:12	82
4:44	72	17:3	173	31:14-15	124
4:44-46	137	17:10	9	31:14-23	87
4:44-49	136, 172	17:16-20	137	31:16-21	124
4:47-49	137	17:18-20	137	31:22-23	124
4:49	72	17:19	137	31:24-30	87
Chapters 4-11	71, 86, 133	19:1 - 21:9	87	31:26-28	124
		19:1-10	137	Chapters 31-33	87
Chapters 4-26	83-84	19:8-10	137	Chapter 32	63, 124, 173
Chapter 5	71	19:14-21	137		
5:1 - 6:3	71, 86, 133	21:1-9	137	32: 16-17	124
5:1 - 26:19	85	21:10 - 22:12	87	32:1-3	125
5:11	81	21:10-14	174	32:1-14	124
5:14	81, 130	22:6-7	128	32:1-43	85, 87
5:23-27	127	22:13-29	87, 174	32:5-6	125
6:4-9	128	23:1	174	32:5-9	124-125
6:4-25	71, 86, 133	23:1-26	87	32:7-9	125
Chapter 7	28, 71, 86	24:1 - 25:4	87	32:7-10	125
7:1-26	86, 133	24:1-4	174	32:7-11	124-125
7:4	173	24:10-13	137	32:7-12	125
7:25	29	24:10-18	137	32:10-11	125
8:1 - 9:6	71, 86, 133	24:13	137	32:10-14	124-125
8:7-10	37, 125, 142	25:5 - 26:15	87	32:13-14	125
8:10	142	25:5-10	174	32:20-27	63, 77
8:11	142-143	26:1-2	128	32:26	170
8:11-16	142	26:16	174	32:44-47	87
9:7 - 10:11	86, 128, 133	26:16-19	87	32:46-4	85
		Chapter 27	132	32:48-52	87
9:15-17	128	27:9-10	85	Chapter 33	87, 125
10:12 - 11:32	71, 86, 133	Chapters 27-30	87	33:1-3	128
		Chapters 27-34	83, 87	33:2-25	125
11:7 - 12:14	138	28:1-68	85	33:26-29	125
11:13-15	173	28:7	28	Chapter 34	125
11:15	173	28:20	173	34:1-12	87
12 - 13	87	28:68-69	128	34:5-6	125
12:1-31	128	28:69	174	34:7-8	125
Chapters 12-26	84, 86, 127	29:1 - 30:20	85	34:9-10	125
		29:5-6	173	34:11-12	125

Judges
2:20-22	63
Chapter 16	29

1 Samuel 2:5 28

2 Samuel 10 28

1 Kings
Chapter 6	27
Chapter 8	26
11:3	28
Chapter 18	29
19:18	28

2 Kings
Chapter 4	28
4:35	29
5:10	29

Isaiah
4:1	29
8:19 - 9:6	149
8:19	150-151, 153
8:19-23	149-150
8:20	150-151
8:20-23	150, 153
8:21	150
8:21-22	151
8:22	150
8:23	150-151
8:32	151
9:1	152, 180
9:1-4	152
9:1-6	149-153
9:2	152
9:2-3	152
9:3	152
9:4	152
9:5	152-153
9:5-6	152
9:6	150, 152-153
Chapter 11	30
11:3-4	31
11:5	32
11:6-10	32
11:7-8	32
Chapter 59	76

Isaiah (cont.)
59:1-8	76
59:1-14	76
59:9-14	76
59:15-18	76
59:15-21	76
59:19	76
59:19-21	91
59:20-21	76

Jeremiah
36:26	95
36:32	95

Ezekiel 40:22 29

Nahum 1 165

Zechariah
1:1-17	49
1:18-21	49
Chapters 1-8	49, 135
2:1	49
2:1-4	49
2:5	49
3:9	29, 49
4:1-14	49, 135, 179
4:2	29, 49
4:4	49
4:7	135
4:10	29, 49
5:1-4	49
5:5-11	49
6:1-8	49

Malachi
3:19-2	138
3:23-24	138
4:1-3	138
4:5-6	138

Psalms
Chapters 1-41	128
Chapter 8	145, 147
8:2	145-146
8:2-3	146
8:2-9	146
8:2-10	146

Psalms (cont.)
8:3	146
8:4	145-146
8:4-5	146
8:6	145
8:6-9	146
8:7	146
8:10	145-146
Chapter 12	27
Chapter 19	94, 147, 149
19:1-2-15	148
19:2	147
19:2-4	148
19:2-5	147
19:2-7	147-148
19:3	147
19:5	147
19:5	148
19:6-11	148
19:7	94
19:8	147
19:8-11	148
19:8-15	147
19:9	147
19:10	147
19:15	147
Chapter 23	11, 14, 36, 123, 134, 143-144
23:4	11, 135
Chapter 34	179
Chapter 37	13
Chapters 42-72	128
45:1	95
Chapter 46	157
Chapter 67	168
72:18-19	91
Chapters 73-89	128
Chapter 79	135, 179
79:12	27
79:1-7	135
Chapter 81	179
Chapter 82	143
82:1	144
82:1-4	143-144
82:2	143
82:2-4	143

Index of Scripture Citations

Psalms (cont.)	
82:5	143-144
82:5-8	143-144
82:6-7	144
82:8	144
Chapter 90	134
90:9	134
90:10	134
90:10-17	134
Chapters 90-106	128
Chapter 91	135
91:1-8	135
91:9	135
91:9-16	135
Chapter 92	179
92:5	134
92:6	134
92:7	134
92:9	134
92:2	134
92:3	134
92:4	134
92:5	134
92:6	134
92:8	134
92:9	134
92:10	134
92:11	134
92:12	134
92:13	134
92:14	134
92:15	134
92:16	134
102:13-23	91
Chapters 107-150	128
Chapter 111	12-13, 79
Chapter 112	12-13, 79
112:9	12
112:10	12
Chapter 119	12-14, 27
119:88	14
119:89	14
119:164	27
139:5	11

Job	
1:1 - 3:1	103
2:11 - 3:1	108
2:11	108-109
2:12	109
2:13	108-109
Chapter 3	108
3:1	108-109
3:2	108-109
6:1	109
9:1	109
12:1	109
42:7-17	103
42:8	29

Proverbs	
Chapter 9	38
9:1	29
24:16	27
31:10-31	13

Ruth 4:15	28

Ecclesiastes	
1:1-11	138-140
1:1-18	138
1:2	138
1:12 - 6:11	140
1:12 - 12:8	139-140
1:12	138
2:1 - 6:8	138
6:9	138-139
6:9-10	139
6:10 - 11:6	138
6:10	139
6:12	139-140
7:1 - 12:8	140
11:7 - 12:14	138
12:8	139
12:9-14	138-140

Lamentations	
Chapter 1	14
Chapter 2	14
Chapter 3	14
Chapter 4	14
Chapter 5	14

Daniel 4	27
Ezra 7:11	95

Nehemiah 9:5	91

1 Chronicles	
2:55	95
Chapter 3	33
27:32	95
28:12-1	168
28:19	118
12:8-10	167

2 Chronicles	
13:10-11	168
29:21	29
34:13	95

Aprocrypha
Wisdom of Solomon
11:21	117

New Testament
Matthew	
Chapter 1	136
1:7-9	136
1:1-17	33
1:17	33
1:18-25	34
Chapter 5	38
5:20	38
5:22	38
5:26	167
5:28	38
5:32	38
5:34	38
5:39	38
5:44	38
12:43-45	30
Chapter 13	26, 37
18:20	175
18:21-22	27
22:23-28	30

Matthew

Chapter 23	38
23:13	38
23:14	38
23:15	38
23:16	167
23:23	38
23:25	38
23:27	38
23:29	38

Mark

6:38	30
8:6	30

Luke

Chapter 2	30
2:25-26	35
11:2-4	36
11:5-12	36
17:3-4	27

John

1:5	151
2:1-11	37
4:46-54	37
5:1-18	37, 136
5:15	136
6:1-15	37
6:16-21	37

John (cont.)

6:35	38
8:12	38
9:1-16	37
10:7	38
10:11	38
11:1-46	37
11:25	38
14:6	38
15:1	38
Chapter 17	120
17:1-3	120
17:1-5	120-121
17:6-8	120
17:7-8	121
17:9-13	120
17:12-13	121
17:14	120
17:14-16	121
17:15-19	120
17:20-24	120
17:25-26	120-121
17:26	121
21:11	12, 80

Acts

2:5-13	165
Chapter 6	30
7:44	178
13:19	28

Romans

Chapter 8	38
8:35	37
11:4	28
12:6-8	38

2 Corinthians

4:7	158

Galatians 4:4 33

Hebrews 8:5 178

James 3:13-18 38

2 Peter

1:21	158
1:6-7	39

Revelation

5:12	39
6:15	39
7:4-8	24
7:12	39
13:17-18	155
Chapter 21	24
21:8	39

www.ingramcontent.com/pod-product-compliance
Lightning Source LLC
Chambersburg PA
CBHW062037220426
43662CB00010B/1538